Classic Confessions

Tell-tale secrets, scandals and sin!

Classic Confessions

Tell-tale secrets, scandals and sin!

SIMON MAYO

Cartoons by Matt

HarperCollins*Publishers*

HarperCollins*Publishers*
77–85 Fulham Palace Road,
Hammersmith, London W6 8JB

First published in Great Britain
in 1994 by HarperCollins*Publishers*

1 3 5 7 9 8 6 4 2

Most of the material in this book originally appeared in
Confessions, Further Confessions and *The Very Worst of Confessions*

A catalogue record for this book is
available from the British Library

ISBN 0 551 02903-X

Printed and bound in Great Britain by
HarperCollinsManufacturing Glasgow

For my little daughter Natasha,
who will of course never do anything
as silly as the crimes in this book.

Contents

Introduction

William Pitt the Younger (1759-1806) was one of this country's most able, talented and witty Prime Ministers. He thought up many fab and groovy ideas including income tax! (5 out of 10), fighting Napoleon (8 out of 10) and uniting Great Britain and Ireland (3 out of 10). When he became Prime Minister in 1783, no one gave him a hope and said it would be all over by Christmas.

Simon Mayo the Elder (0900-1200) is one of this country's most able, talented and witty broadcasters. He has thought up many fab and groovy ideas including joining Radio 1! (9 out of 10), doing the Breakfast Show! (9 out of 10), and inventing Confessions! (must be 10 out of 10). This idea was only intended to last three months and be all over by Christmas.

Five years, four books, 1000s of letters and a TV series later, he (Mayo, not Pitt) can still be found, hunched wearily in a BBC corner, reading through yet more torrid tales of laxative chocolate abuse. None of those (well, hardly any) have made it into this book. This volume has most of the favourites from the first three books, plus some of the best stories from the last 18 months. Flogging a dead horse? Not at all, but that is one of my favourite animal confessions.

As the Good Book says, 'Go and sin no more'. But if you do, do tell me first.

Kids!

You get up in the night to them. You spend all your money on them. You age prematurely for them. And how do they return your love/sleep/youth? By inserting the entire contents of the house into your video machine, by faking injury and illness, smoking, swearing and picking their nose. Plus any one of the following....

Leigh
Lancashire

Dear Simon,

My true confession happened ten years ago when I was twelve years old.

Dad, who had just come out of hospital after having his appendix taken out, was recovering at home. My brother, Steven, who was ten, Mum and I were all in the bedroom watching TV and having coffee and biscuits. Anyway, the biscuits were Lincolns, the ones with pimples on, and after we had eaten a few, my brother went to get another one and found the pimples were all red – the same on another three in the packet.

So Mum sent the packet back to the manufacturer. Two weeks later, a man came to our house full of apologies, and with a load of free products. He explained that the lab technicians had been carrying out tests on the biscuits. The staff had been quizzed, but they were all baffled by it.

Well now I confess to Mum, and the baffled technicians, that it was me who had previously removed them from the packet and coloured them in with a felt-tip pen. Sorry, everyone. Please forgive me!

Yours faithfully

Paul F.

Halesworth
Suffolk

Dear Simon,

I was, for my sins, an 11+ entrant to a grammar school in Surrey then noted for its appalling levels of snobbery and its reluctance to accept that us yobbos from 'the council estate' actually could possess abilities worthy of their consideration. Unless, of course, you played cricket and soccer or were an ace athlete, in which case all sins of breeding were forgiven.

Along with three others in my class, I was overweight and sportingly inept: as a consequence, during games and PE we were segregated from the more athletic by the marvellously sensitive PE teacher Mr Loftus with instructions like: 'Group 1, basketball; group 2, apparatus; you fat boys, medicine ball.'

Medicine balls, as you probably know, are (or were) large leather balls stuffed with very dense wadding. The fat boys' PE lesson consisted of unsupervised throwing of this to each other until 40 minutes were up and Mr L yelled 'Fat boys to the shower now.'

As you may imagine, our gang of four were not too fond of PE or its teacher, and when one day an opportunity arose for revenge, we wasted little time in considering the morals of the issue, or indeed the consequences of our (inevitable) discovery.

One Friday PE lesson in June, it was discovered that the medicine ball had split, but instead of being offered an alternative activity such as sports, we were given a large needle and a thin leather thong and told to stitch it back up. Our first thought was to remove the heavy wadding and replace it with something lighter, thus making our PE a bit less burdensome, but further discussion made us realize the desirability of other stuffings, such as something gooey or malodorous or both. We settled on a dogfish. There were many of these in the biology lab waiting to be turned into displays of nerves, bones and viscera, so obtaining one was a doddle. They were preserved in formaldehyde, quite smelly in its own right, but as the fish got exposed to air its own scent soon asserted itself and we felt confident that, given a weekend, the PE cupboard would niff nicely when opened by Mr L. No sooner decided than acted upon, and the dogfish was procured and entombed in the ball!

The best-laid schemes, etc. . . . . Mr L had his hand broken at a weekend cricket match, and was replaced for the rest of term by a Mr Somebody-or-other who had strange egalitarian ideas of sport which involved everybody doing athletics on the field. The medicine ball lay forgotten in the PE cupboard, its contents liquefying and putrefying, a biology lesson in its own right.

Forgotten, that is, until September, when Mr L, keen to start in again on us 'fat boys' opened the cupboard, was overcome by the stench and was even more overcome by the evil-smelling liquid dogfish which oozed over his hands when he picked up the ball. Needless to say, the culprits were easily identified and brought to book.

I seek forgiveness, not from Mr L, whose reward for insensitivity towards us was well deserved, nor from the dogfish, who at least rotted in peace rather than in pieces, but from the poor school-keeper who had to clean out the PE cupboard afterwards. Mind you, given his age then, he's probably now cleaning up that Great PE Cupboard in the Sky and could get The Boss to do the forgiving direct!!

Peter

P.S. I'm now in the profession upon which I enjoyed my revenge: DON'T EVEN THINK OF IT, CLASS 4M!!!!

Frome
Somerset

Dear Simon,

I have been nursing a terrible secret concerning my home town (Worcester) Cathedral, and now I have been away from Worcester for so long, I feel that I can bring out the awful truth before my fellow men . . .

It is more than twenty years ago, when I was but a Cub Scout, when the Three Counties Scouting organizations convened a massive service and parade through Worcester. Hundreds of Scouts, Guides, Cubs (dyb, dyb), Sea Scouts, etc. etc., plus proud parents descended upon Worcester Cathedral for this service. A few lucky (!) members of various Scout and Cub packs were 'volunteered' to do readings at this service. I was one of them.

I had to recite the Cub Scout Law, not a great literary work, and only three lines about 'doing good deeds', etc. Worcester Cathedral is a big place, so one had to mount the rostrum and spout forth into a mike, which broadcast one's effort throughout the hallowed hall.

I was just a tad scared. The time came, and I wobbled up the rostrum steps, cleared my throat (quietly) and began:

'This is the Cub Scout Law . . .' The mike was off. The front rows heard the mouse-like whisper and giggled.

Undeterred, I switched the mike, and began again . . .

'This is the . . .' Still very quiet. The front rows were in hysterics.

Unbeknown to me, one was supposed to wait for the Deacon to appear with a rod and bow to the reader to indicate your clearance for take-off. He was nowhere to be seen.

I switched the mike back again, and decided that at least the front few rows would definitely hear my speech. I BELLOWED . . .

'THIS IS THE CUB SCOUT LAW . . .' The Deacon had turned on the P.A.

The front row's hair stood on end as the ear-splitting shriek blasted through the Cathedral and loudspeaker cones crackled in overload. Babies started crying, mothers complained about permanent hearing damage.

I finished the speech and backed hastily down the rostrum and hid in my seat.

So, I confess and apologize. Not to the members of the congregation as I'm sure the deafness was only temporary, but to the Friends of Worcester Cathedral, because the beautiful Bell Tower has been crumbling ever since. Visitors to the Cathedral are not allowed under the tower, there is scaffolding everywhere, and many thousands of pounds have been raised to try and rebuild it.

May I plead for forgiveness? I was young and foolish. I did have to wear a woggle and shorts. I only managed the Fireman's badge. I didn't mean any harm . . .

Yours sincerely and with heavy heart

Hove
East Sussex

Dear Simon,

Let me take you back to 1979. At the time I was nine years old and, along with every other nine-year-old boy, I was a fanatical fan of 'Starsky & Hutch'. Every week we would avidly tune in to see our TV heroes in action – except this week.

My father worked abroad during the week as a builder and, as times were hard, my mother worked evenings at the local supermarket stacking shelves. This left my nan to babysit me and my younger brother and sister. Normally I was allowed by my mum to stay up that extra hour to watch 'Starsky & Hutch', but on this rare evening that my nan looked after us, I had received my marching orders just as the programme was about to begin.

After tucking me in, she returned downstairs to the living-room. That was when my plan was hatched. I'd make my way downstairs and pretend to slip. My nan would come to my aid and I would sit with her as she nursed me (as nans do) watching 'Starsky & Hutch' until my mum returned from work.

I crept halfway down the stairs, hit them a few times, let out a few cries and sat clutching my ankle. I waited. Nothing. Then it dawned on me that I hadn't taken into account the fact that my nan was slightly deaf and was watching the TV with the volume on full (as nans do). I tried again, but this time a little louder. Again nothing. So in my frustration I decided that drastic measures were required. I went to the top of the stairs and jumped a few at a time stomping as I landed, screaming 'Ouch'. I then lay at the bottom faking my agony. The living-room door was flung open and my nan ran, well hobbled, towards me. She asked if I was okay. I said, 'Yes, I think so.' Then my plan went horribly wrong. 'Let me get you back to bed,' my nan replied. She wasn't supposed to say that. I had to think quickly and act quicker. As she began to lift me up I let out a howl. 'My neck, I can't move it.'

The panic that ensued was now out of my control. My nan, who by now was hysterical, called my mother at work, who in turn became hysterical and phoned for an ambulance. The ambulance rushed me to the Accident and Emergency department of our local hospital where I was X-rayed. The doctor, surprisingly enough, could find nothing wrong but prescribed a neck-brace should be worn for a couple of weeks, just to be on the safe side.

I never did see that episode of 'Starsky & Hutch', but I did have two weeks off school to recover.

I seek forgiveness for causing my mum so much stress and for keeping her up half the night at A & E and for the stress caused to my dear-departed nan who I never did have a chance to apologize to, not to mention my teacher and all my classmates who had a collection and brought a get-well parcel of sweets 'n' things round to my house.

I hope you see fit to forgive the futile attempts of a small boy to stay up and watch his favourite television programme.

Yours sincerely,

P.B.W.

Swansea

Dear Simon,

I would like to confess something which happened quite a few years ago, when my brother and I lived in Glasgow.

It was a Friday night and we were due to go and stay with my grandmother in London the next day for our summer holiday. My mum was out shopping and my brother had a few friends round from school to say goodbye.

We had a very old-fashioned kitchen with a big range. Above the range was a line where my mum had hung all our undies to air ready for us to take on our hols. Also hanging on the line was my mum's pride and joy, a beautiful pink petticoat, the type worn in those days, made of the stuff that made your dress stick out when you sat down. It was lovely, with lots of lace and pink rosebuds. Well, my brother, who was fifteen at the time, and his friends were in the kitchen – I wasn't allowed in, being much younger, so I spied on them through the crack in the door. I could see them playing with the poker attached to the gas cooker, and burning bits of string which I thought was very naughty of them. I decided I would tell my mum.

My brother decided that it was time everyone went home and while they were getting their coats on, I decided to have a go at lighting the poker myself. There I was, gaily waving this flame about when all of a sudden – whoosh! My mum's lovely pink petticoat was melting on to the floor. I put the poker back and ran down to the front door and said 'I can smell something burning, can't you?' They all sniffed and ran back to the kitchen, where by now all our underclothes were alight.

Imagine the scene. You have just picked up your wife from outside the supermarket after having had a hard day at the office to be greeted by a number of frantic teenagers carrying buckets and bowls of burning socks, ties and various other items of underwear to the bathroom. Well, my mum screamed and my dad blew a gasket. After a frantic half hour, they had the situation under control. My brother said a sheepish 'goodbye' to his friends, and then we were interrogated. As I didn't want to get smacked and I didn't particularly want to get my brother into too much trouble. I decided that I would blame his friend Steven, who I didn't really like anyway. I said that I saw him playing with the poker in the kitchen and to my surprise my brother backed me up.

Well, the end of the story is that Steven got banned for life from the house, my brother was grounded for quite some time and me – well, I got a whole load of new underclothes.

This incident has always been on my mind and I'd just like to say 'sorry' to Steven, wherever he is, to my brother and my parents, especially to mum who was so upset at having lost her beautiful petticoat – not even the elastic was left – but she did get a new kitchen out of it.

Barbara

Carlisle

Dear Father Simon,

Seventeen years ago, when I was the tender age of four, ten minutes of innocent play has resulted in my conscience being darkened ever since.

At the time, we lived on a dairy farm on the outskirts of Carlisle, and with no brothers or sisters then, very often there was very little to do, apart from watching the greatest team on earth, Carlisle United, every Saturday afternoon.

One summer's day, bored with my sand-pit, Tiny Tears and Tonka Trucks, I ventured into a field to play with the cows. The cows drank from an old cast iron bath in the middle of the field, although at the time I believed it was where they had their daily dip. Having watched my mum wallow in a deep Radox bath, wouldn't it be lovely, I thought, if the cows could have a luxurious bubble bath too? I was sure my mum wouldn't appreciate me using her bubble bath for the cows, so I decided to search in the farm sheds for some. Success! A lovely container of green bubble bath, marked with red lettering. I carried it back over the field to the bath and poured the liquid in, mixing it carefully with a stick.

My bubble bath was forgotten about until several days later, when a convoy of vets, police cars and local newspaper reporters arrived at our farm. Apparently, my 'bubble bath' was a container of concentrated weedkiller, and had resulted in the death of one cow and the severe illness of three others. The police suspected two local characters who had recently been released on bail on charges of arson at another farm, resulting in these men being brought in to the station for questioning, but later being released. My parents and I had our photo taken for the local rag, with me holding the empty container of 'bubble bath' – I think the cutting is somewhere in our attic.

I now wish to seek forgiveness for my actions seventeen years ago – forgiveness from my parents for their financial loss and disturbed state of mind (permanent), from the police for their wasted time, from the two men who were questioned by the police, and forgiveness from you. You should know that I am now a respectable law student, totally against animal cruelty and a member of Greenpeace.

Anxiously awaiting your decision,

Erica

Plymouth
Devon

Dear Simon,

Unlike some of the seedy confessions that you get, this is a simple tale of an ambitious, yet somewhat spoilt child of seven years old, many years ago.

Well the spoilt brat was me, and this is how the story goes: you know in schools there is always one child who wants to be blackboard monitor, takes part in all the pantomimes, enters every sports day and is generally the school goody goody, well that was me, and believe it or not, even though that is a confession in itself, it does go on . . .

Luckily, I was always chosen for school events BUT, strangely enough, I was never able to enter the swimming gala. Why? Because I couldn't swim! Well, I wasn't going to let that minor detail spoil my chance of being in the limelight, and when the PE teacher was picking sprogs for different events in the swimming gala, in the glorious summer of 1976, something possessed me, I felt my hand shoot up, and I found myself entered in the one-width breast stroke, and I only had one week to learn to swim!!

I rushed home to tell my mummy the good news, and I must say she was quite surprised, as she knew very well that I had the buoyancy of a rather large brick! But she did agree to come along and cheer me on!

The day of the gala arrived, and it was going 'swimmingly'!! It was time for my event. If you wanted, you could dive in, but I didn't want to push my luck, so I started in the water, the whistle blew, and we were off.

You may be thinking WOW! she learnt to swim in just one week, but no I hadn't, although I had perfected my swim-hop, which involved hopping and kicking alternately across the pool, creating such a splash nobody would ever know I wasn't actually swimming. All the children, parents and teachers were cheering and jumping up and down, except my mum, who was staring open-mouthed. She knew what I was up to, as I had conned her out of 50p several months before, when I had pulled the same trick on her, but had been proved to be a fraud. Mummy was even more shocked when I won, and I was presented with a lovely trophy . . . was I chuffed or what!

I just thanked my lucky stars that I had been in the shallow end, otherwise I could have drowned. I have never seen my mum blush so much as when the headmistress, Mrs Fern, said, 'You must be very proud of her'.

I hope my mum can forgive me, and if the pupils of Langley Primary School remember the occasion, perhaps they will forgive me too? You will be glad to know that I have learnt to swim, though Sharron Davies, I am not!

All the best . . .

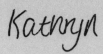

West Sussex

Dear Simon,

I have a confession, which dates all the way back to when I was five years old! Do you remember, Simon, the games we used to play at kindergarten? Games such as 'It' or 'Cops and Robbers' or 'Stick in the Mud'?

One such game which was a favourite in our school was 'Choo-choo train'. To begin with, a line of about three or four people, with the dinner lady in front, would all put their hands on the person in front's waist. We would then putter about the playground making 'choo-choo train' noises. This would usually go on until the end of playtime, during which time the train gradually gained length. At the end of break the 'choo-choo train' might be as long as about thirty or so little five-year-olds.

The story begins one playtime, when nothing seemed to be happening. I was very bored and I approached a dinner lady on duty in the playground. 'Let's start a choo-choo train!' I said eagerly. 'Good idea!' she said, and a little two-person train started choo-chooing around the playground. It wasn't long before I felt someone else grab hold of my waist, and felt the presence of someone else grab the waist of the boy behind me.

Now, that's where I thought it would end: a choo-choo train of only four or so people, even though the whole place was echoing with choo-choo noises. So, you can imagine my surprise when a little later I decided to turn my head to see who was behind me. A line of about fifty or so people greeted my eyes. A mega choo-choo train! At that time I was very shy, and the thought of being at the front of a train that large completely put me out. I did the only thing which came to mind: step out of the line.

I am truly sorry to say that it was not only the boy who was behind me who fell flat on his face, but all the other fifty or so youngsters who made up this 'choo-choo train' also found themselves being toppled to the ground with a tremendous amount of G-Force, and speed.

I was mortified, but not half as much as the dinner lady who had originally led this train; she still to this day thinks it was all her own fault for going too fast in the first place.

Yours,

Michael

Dear Father Mayo,

My confession dates back to the early days of decimalization when I was only a wee young lad. Being a very inquisitive and daft child, I did what everyone of my age would have done with a new 2p piece – I swallowed it!

After the initial panic of turning blue and the apparent lack of breath, I calmed myself down and decided to seek help. I rushed home and told my mother, who insisted on a trip to the local hospital. Sitting in the waiting room, with children with saucepans on their heads and buttons stuck up their noses (just the usual, quite normal day at Sunderland General Hospital) I awaited my fate.

After what seemed hours I was taken into a room with more gadgets than the Starship Enterprise and asked to undress and lie on the table. 'Don't worry son, I'm only giving you an X-ray,' explained the doctor. 'It won't hurt a bit and is completely safe,' he said as he hurried behind a lead wall.

A few minutes later he announced what I already knew, 'You've swallowed a 2p piece.' 'Amazing', I thought. 'What will we have to do?' asked my worried mother. 'No surgery is required', the doctor replied. 'Just let nature take its course.' It wasn't until I got home that I was informed what that meant. From then on I had to do the obvious in a bucket until the 2p was found, a job my mother thought best suited to . . . Dad! For nearly two weeks he searched the contents of the bucket, sometimes twice a day, until the 2p was finally discovered, much to his relief.

Now after all these years I have decided to confess all. I have never had the heart, or guts, to come clean and admit that I found the 2p on the same day I returned from the hospital and decided to plant a 2p in the bucket when I could see Dad had had enough. Can you forgive me for this dreadful deed?

Will my dad forgive me?

Will the Royal Mint forgive me?

Please end my suffering as I can't look at a 2p piece without filling with guilt.

Yours Owning-up-ingly,

Gary
(Age 25 3(4))!!

High Wycombe

Dear Simon,

I must confess to something that has been with me for 18 years.
    I was aged 11 and I arrived home from school one day in proud possession of two large magnets a friend had ripped out of the back of two old and very big hi-fi speakers. On arriving home my brother, three years my senior, told me about a wonderful experiment he had done in his physics class several weeks earlier.

    Our television set was no more than a few days old. The black-and-white one had been playing up so, at great expense, Dad had gone out and bought the very latest all-singing-all-dancing colour TV set. They were still a bit of a novelty so ours was treated with the greatest of respect . . . until now!

    My brother showed me how to distort and jump the picture using my strong magnets. It was fantastic. Peter Purvis and the whole 'Blue Peter' crew jumped and bent themselves all out of shape, changing colour like chameleons. We squealed with delight as our heroes proceeded to look so stupid.

    After the fun had calmed down, we noticed the TV hadn't. We switched it on and off, changed channels, even the 'Magpie' lot on the other side were all wrong!

    We switched the telly off and listened to the radio and awaited Dad. He arrived home and went insane. We pleaded our innocence, claiming 'it just went like that when we switched it on'! He then interrogated us individually to see if our stories tallied. Fortunately they did.

    The TV repair man was called. The day before he arrived, the set mysteriously fixed itself but he came to check it out anyway. 'It's OK,' he said, 'these models sometimes do that, when they're settling in' (winking at me and my brother). Needless to say my Dad sent the television back and never bought another of that make again.

    Sorry, Dad, you weren't going insane, it *was* me and my brother. Are we forgiven?

            Cheers mate . . . ,

                Craig

Peterborough

Dear Simon,

I have decided to confess my darkest secret.

My family originate from Sheffield. I am the eldest of three sisters and life was reasonably happy for my next sister down and me until one fateful 18th July, when our youngest sister, Anne, arrived. She was the child about whom everyone who gazed into her pram exclaimed, 'Isn't she beautiful!'

Now this carried on throughout her babyhood, whilst she was a toddler, a mixed infant and through her junior school (still carries on to this day, Simon, actually). As you might imagine, my other sister and I grew mighty fed up with all this adulation of our youngest sister, but it wasn't until Anne reached the age of about twelve or thirteen that we successfully managed to plot our revenge. Our revenge revolved around her being asleep, darkness and a bottle of trick tan (the sort that makes you go orange overnight).

The plan was hatched. When Anne went to sleep (for someone so beautiful she didn't half snore like a pig) my sister and I smeared her face, arms and hands with fake tan. Next morning when she woke up she made her usual trip to the mirror to admire the perfect reflection and screamed in horror when she saw her face all blotchy and brown – not to mention the arms and hands attractively patterned to match. Our parents were called and were suitably horrified while my other sister and I had to feign our shock whilst trying incredibly hard not to laugh (revenge is so sweet, not to mention hysterically funny).

Well, baby sister was dispatched to the doctor who could see no reason for the strange skin pigmentation. Our campaign carried on for some months with each recurrence of the blotches more baffling than the previous attack. In short, Simon, I would now like to apologize to my sister Anne, our family doctor, and to the skin specialist at the Northern General Hospital.

No, it wasn't some strange skin condition – it was me, my sister and a bottle of Tanfastic. Can we be forgiven?

Yours sincerely,

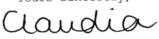
Claudia

Leeds

Dear Father Simon,

I was not even a twinkle in my mother's eye when both my parents went to Tanzania as medical missionaries after finishing medical school. However, the twinkle appeared and – not much later – so did I.

Our little village of Mvumi (which means 'wind' by the way) was indeed little, and so it was with great excitement that the local church welcomed our bishop one Sunday, who arrived in a sophisticated four-wheel drive Land-Rover about the time that I was three and my chum, Christopher Keith, about four.

You must understand, Kind Father, that in Tanzania it is very hot. Even when it is cold it is hot, and the day that the bishop came was a scorcher. It was on days like this that Chris and I had found that when we were fortunate enough to come across such a rare and luxurious item as a bicycle – or even a motorbike – we could send a soothing breeze across our sweating brows by pressing a certain point on the tyres.

Imagine our delight when, that scorching hot Sunday morning, we found in our own village a vehicle with four huge tyres – each packed with refreshing, cool air. We eagerly set to work easing our discomfort, and it was with great disappointment that we drained the last hiss of air and had to leave.

I beg the forgiveness of Bishop Madinda who returned to find his vehicle four inches lower than he had left it, and of whoever had to work in the African heat pumping up the tyres with a foot pump. I also ask that my sins be forgiven by my parents, who had to face such an early rebellion against the church, and by Chris on whom I grassed and whose parents were a lot more angry than mine were with me.

Yours coolly,

Matthew

Swindon

Dear Simon,

I've carried my confession for many years and now finally I feel it's time to reveal all and rid me of my sins!

We were moving house. Everything was carefully packed into boxes and stored in our dining room. As my parents were out at the time, I decided to ask a friend round to play, but after she came round we became bored and restless as all of my games had been packed away and out of reach. That's when we decided to raid the kitchen cupboards. We found nothing exciting except an `Angel Delight', so feeling quite hungry we whipped the mix up as fast as we could. Mum could have walked in at any second.

When we had finished mixing, the pudding still looked rather boring. That's when I had a great idea! I could remember seeing some Hundreds and Thousands in a box right at the back of all the items my parents had already packed. I quickly hurried to the box and pulled them out. As I did, the lid came off and out flew hundreds and thousands of the Hundreds and Thousands!

In a panic I shouted at my friend to go and stall my mother (who was due back at any moment) while I tidied up. As I was hoovering and struggling round the boxes with my arms going frantically everywhere, I heard a ripping sound. Slowly I looked round and a wave of horror swept over me. In my panic to tidy up I had put the end of the hoover through the canvas of my parents' prized painting they had bought while living in Singapore.

I finished hoovering and for the rest of the day was a nervous wreck. All night I prayed my parents wouldn't notice their favourite painting had been defaced (they didn't!). The next day after school I took it down to the nearest field and threw it as far as I could into someone's garden.

A few weeks later we moved to our new house and after several days of unpacking I overheard my dad asking my mum where she had put the painting. She said that she didn't know, but she definitely remembered the removal man putting it into his van. After several hours of searching for it my dad was on the phone to the removal company saying he would never use them again and that he would refuse to pay his bill. He even threatened to go and see a solicitor. The removal company took details of our move and said the matter would be dealt with and the driver reprimanded.

Meanwhile, I sat in the dining room listening to the conversation with a smug grin on my face. For a moment I felt sorry for the removal van driver, and how with my help he was one step nearer the dole queue. But now the time has come to ask for forgiveness from my parents, for I demolished their prized picture, and also to the removal man, who swore on his life he never took it.

Do you forgive me?

A. Nonymous

Bless me dear Simon,

Whilst in my third year of school I was set a poetry assignment and as usual I had left it until the last minute. I was much happier listening to my new album of the unforgettable legends of pop history, the most excellent 'Then Jericho' whilst hopelessly swooning over the cover photograph of the lead singer Mark Shaw – the most beautiful man since Morten Harkett. Thus distracted to this extent I was unable to concentrate on my poem due in the next day.

Whilst glancing over the sleeve notes containing the lyrics I was struck, nay moved, by their inspirational qualities and that was when the idea cunningly infiltrated my common sense. To avoid the risk of detention from my English teacher I foolishly copied down the lyrics to a whole song all about a woman being attacked by a hitchhiker but after my clever alterations it read more as an angry piece of social commentary about the vulnerability of women on our streets.

The result from my teacher was more than I had anticipated. Not only did my poem come top of the class, I was forced to read it out at the school assembly. Worse was still to come, however . . .

One day I was called to the staffroom to be informed that my poem had secretly been entered for the Cadbury's National Children's Poetry Competition and had won. The prize included the publication of the forgery in a book full of other poems; real poems written by honest children, plus the inclusion of the thing in a travelling national exhibition of children's art.

I should have said something then really, but the other prize of a huge bar of chocolate had inevitably meant my tastebuds had hijacked my conscience and prevented me from telling my proud teacher I was a fraud. It was already too late. The local press had hurriedly been informed of the fact that our school, notorious for anything but culture, had produced a prize-winning poet. So there I was smiling out from every local paper in the county holding my poem and certificate with a 'proud but poetically sensitive' expression on my face.

My parents were a complete nightmare. They were so chuffed at the revelation that the family had produced what they saw as the bard of the twentieth century. Everyone knew about it. I was in an impossible situation. I could not let down my school, my parents and the whole population of the village, could I?

The consequences of owning up were far too depressing to seriously contemplate. Would they tear out the pages that my poem was on in all the books? Would all the local papers issue a press release or even worse write an investigative report into the scandal of the plagiaristic poet who won a poetry competition with song lyrics from a crappy teen pin-up band? Hurriedly, I ate the chocolate prize before they could repossess it and then had nightmares about the boss of Cadbury's making me vomit up the prize as a punishment. The sad thing was that I had started to believe I had actually written the thing myself and continued to do so for a long time. I even included the 'poem published in a book' bit on my UCCA form. In short I was living a complete lie.

I come to you then, Simon, to grant me absolution from this sin. It was just three weeks ago that I finally and fully confessed this wicked deed, this smudge on my past, this stain on my otherwise unbesmirched character.

I would like to take this opportunity to do two things. Firstly to apologize to everyone who believed I was the next poet laureate, especially my parents and my English teacher, and to 'Then Jericho' for winning greater acclaim than they ever did for those lyrics and for not sharing my chocolate prize with them. Secondly, I would beg you, dear Simon, not to inform my parents or the Board of Copyright if you discover my identity. Do you think three Hail Marys will be enough?

Yours

H.

Leicestershire

Dear Simon,

My confession starts fourteen years ago when I was a very easily led fourteen-year-old. I had just joined the smoking club at school, which consisted of four of my friends and myself. We used to go off around the bike sheds or down the train embankment which led on to the school playing fields for a crafty smoke. I'd been in the club for two days and I was told that it was my turn to buy the fags tomorrow if I wanted to stay in the infamous club. So I agreed and was in deep thought for the rest of the day as to how I would finance my subscription.

It was 3 November, two days before bonfire night and three days before my younger sister's seventh birthday. I had saved up my pocket money for three weeks and had enough to buy some fireworks, which I had purchased the evening before from the Indian shop. All my money had gone – what was I going to do about my ciggie subscription? Nothing came to mind, so I forgot all about it and thought smoking was for divvies.

The next morning I awoke first, surprisingly early for me as I was normally a very difficult child to get out of bed in the morning. I made my way downstairs and saw a pink envelope peeking through the letter box. I went to investigate and saw it was addressed to my sister. 'An early birthday card,' I thought. I checked the postmark out of curiosity, saw it was postmarked Stenhousemuir and knew it was from my aunty way up north. 'She sent me some money for my birthday,' I recalled and thought that there must be some money in this card for my sister. Then it clicked: subscription fees for my newfound pastime! I thought about it long and hard for at least thirty seconds and came to the conclusion that my sister would only spend it on sweets, which would undoubtedly cause tooth decay and in turn cause my sweet dear sister pain and distress whilst sat in the dentist's chair – plus my friends were more important than my sister – so in my school bag went the card.

On the way to school that morning I took the card out, opened it up and, as expected, there lay a crisp Scottish £1 note. 'Happy birthday, sister!' I shouted and proceeded towards the aforementioned Indian shop. After spending ten minutes explaining to the proprietor that the £1 note was legitimate currency, I carried on my way to school with my smokes in my pocket, feeling very clever.

As I crashed my fags at first break, it suddenly dawned on me what I had done. Inhaling the menthol flavour smoke, I was violently sick, just as the 10.35 a.m. Leicester to London train went by. Was it the smoke, or was it my guilt getting its own back on behalf of my sister?

Every time I smell cigarette smoke I get a real sense of guilt and I also feel very bilious to my stomach. Needless to say, I am no longer a smoker.

Please give me absolution, as I think fourteen years is a long time to suffer.

Every 6 November my sister gets spoilt by me, so I have made it up to her, but the guilt still remains.

Pete

Somewhere in Wales

Dear Simon,

Please hear my confession about a 'mishap' which has weighed heavy on my troubled mind for a number of years. I'm twenty-five now and reasonably grown up, although some might argue that point because of a somewhat, shall we say, 'alternative' sense of humour.

My confession goes back to the time when I was around seven years of age. I was dragged out shopping by my mother one packed Saturday morning and, like most mothers, mine used to stand and chat to friends for ages leaving the hapless child (i.e. me) holding on to her hand feeling thoroughly bored. Anyway, she'd stopped to talk to this woman in one of the local stores, rather close to the top of the escalator.

Having stood there for around ten minutes getting totally cheesed off and being told about forty times to stand still/stop fidgeting, I spied something which struck me as a potential source of amusement. There, tucked away at the top of the escalator under the rotating rubber handrail was a red circle which said 'Emergency Stop'.

A swift calculation in my devious little mind sussed that I could reach this red circle using the tip of my umbrella without bringing any unnecessary attention my way. Bearing in mind that this escalator was reasonably full and could possibly cause quite serious injury, I pushed the button.

Instead of grinding to a steady halt this thing hurled the unsuspecting shoppers to the floor with a commendable amount of G-Force. It was chaos! Grannies were headbutting the people directly in front of them, and those menacing shopping baskets on wheels that most old folk have (usually in tartan) were demonstrating their remarkable hidden talents at administering puncture wounds.

Mother, my mother's friend and I looked on in horror (or mock horror in my case). The icing on the cake to this tale is that amidst all this pandemonium, at the bottom of the stairs could be seen a young lad being given the slapping of his life by his irate mother (one of those mothers whose every word was accompanied by a sharp clout), who was screaming, 'What have I told you before about touching things that don't belong to you?'

Do you think I could possible be forgiven?

Lots of Love,

F.

Birmingham

Dear Simon,

I've done plenty of wrong things in my time, but there is only one that I feel really guilty about.

I was about ten, and my brother, Keven, would have been six. It wasn't long after Christmas, Mum and Dad had bought Keven a space hopper that year, and to save having to blow it up and let it down all the time it was kept in the only space available – the airing cupboard.

I don't know what possessed me, but each time I went to the airing cupboard and looked at this space hopper, my fingertips started to itch and I had naughty thoughts!

I had to put myself out of my misery. So one day I took a pin, and strolled to the airing cupboard. Instead of sticking it completely through the hopper, my conscience only allowed me to price the surface.

I went to bed that evening feeling relieved and secretly thinking I wouldn't have pricked it hard enough to harm it anyway.

The next day my poor little brother ran to the cupboard, full of excitement and eager to play on his space hopper. Only it had shrunk. The tears on his face and the look of disappointment were too much for me to bear – I hid that day. Mum consoled Keven and explained that he'd probably space-hopped on some broken glass somewhere.

Well, Kev, it'll be your twenty-first birthday in December, and I promise I'll get you a space hopper just like the one you had which I destroyed.

I've never been to confession before, but I feel a lot better now. I may start making this confession lark a habit!

Yours sincerely,

Jerry

Glasgow

Dear Simon,

You might think that nativity plays are the very epitome of Christmas – children sweet and angelic acting out that first Christmas story, glowing faces, proud parents and warm hearts. Most of this is usually true, but at St James Primary School in 1967 things got slightly out of hand.

In our school it was always the top infants class that got to perform the traditional play. Even though we were young the jostling for the best parts started early. Unsurprisingly the roles of Mary and Joseph were the most sought after, followed by the three kings, then came the shepherds and various assorted angels, cattle and so on. As I had played the part of the Pied Piper in a school assembly three months previously I have to admit that I fancied my chances of getting Joseph or a gold-bearing king at least.

Unfortunately for me and my best mate Darren, we were caught throwing our school potatoes at the class weed who was called Tom. The consequences of this harmless event were calamitous. I neither got the role of Joseph nor a king nor a shepherd but that of third innkeeper. I was truly gutted. Third innkeeper? It didn't even merit a mention in the programme, or duplicated sheet to be precise. How could I impress my fellow nine-year-olds as a pathetic one-line-only innkeeper? For the record my words were as follows: 'Sorry, we've no room.' Hardly going to impress the school, was it? To make things worse, the boy who teased my sister for having a big nose got the part of Joseph, and got to rehearsals with the delectable Jennifer Wilkes who was selected to play Mary. All us grown up nine-year-olds fancied her, well as much as a nine-year-old can anyway.

Revenge was clearly called for. There were three performances of our nativity play and I decided that it was the last one, on Friday after-noon, with all the parents in dutiful attendance, that was to be the target of my shockingly well-planned spite. So the scene was set. The stage as I recall looked a picture – Bethlehem AD O. The First Christmas. A nervous Mary and frightfully overacting Joseph approach the first inn; towels on heads and tied dressing gowns about them. 'Is there any room at the inn?' intoned Joseph. 'Sorry, we're full,' says innkeeper 1. On a few steps. 'Is there any room at this inn?' says Joseph again. 'Sorry, we're full tonight,' says innkeeper 2. And on they come to my inn. I've been waiting.

Now I have to say in my defence that I didn't know the meaning of what I was about to say. It was something I'd heard one of the top years say. I knew it was a naughty word but that was it. Back to the stage. Knock knock. 'Is there any room at the inn, please?' says the dreadful Joseph. And in my best acting voice I said, 'No. Bugger off!'

Looking back, I suppose it could have been worse. But not at the time. To say that there was an audible intake of breath is an understatement. To say I got a belting is an understatement. Needless to say this was the end of my acting career and I'm now a supermarket manager who tells his staff off for swearing.

Yours in humble supplication,

TOM

Inverness

Dear Simon,

When I was ten, I had a horrendous teacher, a spinster who had no empathy for children. She made life miserable for anyone who was not one of her special pets. Instead of explaining a subject slowly and patiently when it wasn't understood, she would repeat herself, increasing the volume until her face was purple with rage. Over the years she destroyed the confidence of countless children and reduced many to tears.

Our class project that year was on the Tudors and, by coincidence, this was at the same time as the raising of the *Mary Rose*.

One morning I found a burnt cornflake in my cereal bowl and Dad joked that it looked like a piece of the Mary Rose. So I wrapped the cornflake in cotton wool, put it in a jewellery box and took it to school.

When I reached the class, the teacher waited ten minutes before acknowledging that my hand was up. Finally, exasperated, she demanded to know what was so important. I showed her the cornflake, claiming it was a part of the *Mary Rose* which my (fictitious) aunt in Portsmouth had acquired when the ship was moved to dry dock.

She actually believed me and passed the charred cereal around the class, making sure that nobody so much as breathed on the 'precious piece of history'.

At playtime she tried to insist on locking it in her drawer for safekeeping. I think she really wanted to show it off in the staffroom! But I escaped this by pretending that I had to give it to my sister to show her class. As soon as I was outside, when nobody was looking, I threw it in the bin.

I was so terrified of being found out that I had a 'tummy ache' for the whole of the rest of the week.

As far as I know, that teacher still believes that the piece of burnt cornflake was a tiny remnant of Henry VIII's favourite flagship.

All I can say is that if I could turn the clock back . . . I would think of something worse.

Please read this out as it would ease my conscience consid-
erably and hopefully give my old classmates a laugh.

Yours faithfully,

Elizabeth

Strood
Kent

Dear Simon,

I'm so glad that you have started a confessional service, because it allows me to admit something I did which I've never had the courage to confess before.

Some twelve years ago, I did an awful thing. You see, being the grand old age of ten, I felt that my bicycle was too small and babyish for me. To give you some idea what this bike was like, it was called a 'Zippy' – yes, that's right, after the character in 'Rainbow'.

Well, I nagged and nagged my parents for a new bike, but to no avail. Their argument was that there was nothing wrong with the one I had, and I could wait a few years before I got a new one.

All I could think about was getting a new bike, so I decided to take things into my own hands. My younger sister was only a baby and once a week I was sent to the shops at the end of our road to fetch baby milk. On one such visit, I noticed that behind the shops it was very overgrown with weeds and nettles about knee high. An idea formed in my mind.

Bit by bit I began to dismantle my bike. Each week a nut or bolt or screw would mysteriously disappear, until finally, one day, I arrived home pushing what was left of my old bike. I pretended to be most distraught and told my parents that somehow my bike had just simply fallen apart. I must have been convincing because they believed me.

Sure enough, my wicked plan worked and a week later I was presented with a brand new 'grown-up' bike. I feel really awful about this now and I've never admitted what terrible lengths I went to so I could get a new bike. We have since moved, but if they ever develop the piece of land behind the shops, they will come across enough parts of a bike to build a new one!

I'm sorry, Mum and Dad. I hope I can be forgiven.

from

KAREN

Big Kids

Having survived chapter one and the excesses of the infants, let's move up a grade. Same kind of kids, same kind of crimes but now with two added ingredients: spite and alcohol.

Somewhere in Berkshire

Dear Simon,

I have been forced to write this confession, but anonymity must be maintained as it is so bad.

Some years ago I went to Amsterdam on holiday with a friend, purchased some illegal leaves and smuggled them back into this country. That is a confession in itself, but what follows is far, far worse!

I was informed that the seeds on the leaves could be cultivated if germinated in a damp tissue and left on my bedroom window sill, so there they remained. A couple of years later, having been away at college, I was chatting to my parents about 'Mr Jones', the well-respected Headmaster, JP, Charity Organizer and all-round community 'good guy' in our town, when my mother commented how 'green-fingered' he was and revealed that she had given the seeds on my bedroom window sill to him! My spine froze. I was devastated. I imagined the headlines in the papers . . .

HEAD GROWS OWN DOPE

So please, if you are a Headmaster in the north-west of England, cut down the now twelve-foot plant with the spiky leaves – it's illegal!

This is a true confession.

Anon

P.S. Can I be forgiven?

Dear Father Simon,

I feel the time is right to confess my woeful tale.

It all started back in my student days as a keen engineering student at Nottingham Poly. During the first term of every year, the rugby club organized a toga party, which took place about midway through the term.

The party would start in a well-known pub near the poly, before going on to a night club on the other side of the city centre.

On the night of the great event, there we all were, wrapped in our bedding, consuming large quantities of beer at an alarming rate. As the evening went on, a few of us decided it was time to head off for the night club, and stop for some food on the way.

Walking along the road, we came across every drunk student's dream: road-works. We could not resist the brightly coloured traffic cones or flashing lights, and soon we were playing rugby in the middle of the road with the aforementioned articles.

After a short time, a very irate man leaned out of an office window across the road and shouted, 'Oi! What the (blank) do you think you're doing?' Without saying a word, one of our party walked up to the front of the building, turned so his back faced the office, then lifted up his toga, as some sort of salute to the irate man. Next thing you know, we were all doing the same thing in a long line down the pavement.

After what can only have been a few seconds, I walked up to the main doors of the office to see who the building belonged to. I returned to the rest of the party who were standing around laughing at the event and calmly told them who owned the building. Yes, you've guessed it! The sign said: Nottingham Constabulary Headquarters. We then ran off down the road and into the shopping centre, needless to say very quickly.

In lectures the next day, one of the gang was absent. That evening we went round to his house, expecting to find him slightly the worse for wear, caused by the previous night's beer intake. He wasn't there! In fact, nobody had seen him since he had left the night before to go to the party!

We left the house and headed back home. As we walked down the road, we saw in the distance a youth running along the road like he was Linford Christie, wearing nothing but a sheet draped on his body. As he got nearer we recognized him as our missing member.

As he had been walking home from his girlfriend's in the early hours, he had been picked up by the police. It turned out that the irate man that shouted at us was a Chief Inspector, and had interviewed our chum all day trying to track down the unruly individuals who had shown a complete disregard for authority.

I ask for forgiveness not for our party and the fun we had, but because of the interrogation forced upon this lad by the law.

Yours repentantly,

Mark

Dear Simon,

After listening to the True Confessions of others, I felt that I had to write to bare my soul, hoping at last to free myself from the burden of guilt that I have carried for the last four years.

I was living with my Aunt Margaret in Stubbins, Lancashire, and had been left in charge of the family home after my parents had moved to Norfolk. I had stayed on in Lancashire because we had decided I should finish my schooling — I was sixteen, in my final year at school, and taking exams.

My family were sending me a monthly allowance, some for me and some for Aunt Margaret for looking after me. But I was sixteen, discovering life and my allowance was soon used up. So, finding myself skint, what was I to do?

At this moment I would like to ask my parents, 'What do you think happened to the two bikes (mine and my sister's), the drill and the building tools? The very same items that you searched the house and garden for, and finally claimed for on the insurance?'

Well, both bikes went to a mate, and the drill and building tools went to a mate's mate's dad's mate. These items made a total of £85, and I was able once more to enjoy the style of life to which I had become accustomed.

I would like to apologize to my parents, my sister and the insurance company, and all I can offer in my defence is that when you're young and living life in the fast lane, you have to take chances.

Yours sincerely,

C.R.H.

P.S. I was also offered £15 for the washer/dryer, but I thought that wasn't enough.

Northampton

Dear Father Mayo,

I'm writing to confess a dastardly deed that occurred some thirteen years ago. It all started with my father being a rather avid fossil collector. The family were often spirited off to weird and wonderful places in the world — like mid Wales — to look for fossils. My father had a very impressive collection of bits of dinosaurs in rocks. Big deal, I thought, but they were obviously good to my dear daddy.

Anyway, when I heard of a fossil day coming up at lower school, I eagerly begged Dad to lend me all his best fossils, so I might take them in and show off. As you can guess he said no, and rather bluntly!

What could I do? The day of the big event was drawing rapidly near, and I still had no fossils. All my pleading to Father was in vain. I was stuck, until my little brain hit upon the idea of theft. Yes, I would pinch a heap of fossils on the morning of the event, hope Daddy didn't notice, and replace them before he came home that evening. Perfect. What could possibly go wrong?

The morning of the day came, and I arose early. I crept downstairs to the fossil cabinet, and stood debating on what to take. I didn't want to take so much that it was obvious I'd pinched some, but I wanted to take something spectacular. I actually took a Plesiosaurus's (or something like that) tooth. This dino's muncher was my dad's pride and joy.

When I arrived at school, brandishing a dinosaur's tooth, as opposed to all the other kids' shells and stuff, I got a wonderful reception. I was the centre of attention, for a whole twenty minutes, before a teacher took the tooth to put it on display. As you can imagine, I was fairly concerned about the tooth, and I made the teacher promise faithfully that no harm would come to it. So I was left toothless in the playground, wondering if I'd done the right thing. I was disturbed by the noise from a small crowd of kids behind me. The centre of attraction was now a small brightly coloured bouncy ball belonging to a fellow playmate named Craig. The ball was fantastic, it would bounce for ever, once hurled at the ground. I soon forgot about my tooth, and by the time we heard the bell for lessons, I had decided that I wanted a bouncy ball more than anything. I approached Craig during number counting (as maths was called in them days!), and asked if he'd swap it for my pencil case? No. My sandwiches? No. My Dairylea slice? Still no. Hang on, what about my tooth? 'Oh, I suppose so,' was the reply from Craig. I waited until break, then ran to the hall where the display was. Sneaking my way past the teachers, I managed to retrieve my tooth without being spotted. I ran back to Craig, and the goods exchanged hands. I was then quite content for the rest of the day – until I remembered my father. Oh dear! I thought, though not using those exact words. I excused myself from my lesson, saying I 'needed to go' very urgently, and ran off in a desperate attempt to find Craig. I was duly informed by a teacher that Craig had gone home sick at lunchtime.

The teacher, obviously sensing that I was fairly distressed, enquired what was wrong. I told her that Craig had my tooth, but I failed to mention the fact that we had a bargain involving a rubber ball. The teacher assumed that Craig had pinched the tooth and done a runner. She assured me that he would be dealt with very severely when he returned to school. In the meantime I was to go home and tell my parents what had happened. So I went home as usual, and told my father the unlikely tale. I was told, very sternly, to retrieve the tooth by the end of the week or I was in deep trouble.

The next day Craig was back at school, and only too happy to swap back, as he was bored with the tooth. Five minutes later, Craig was spotted, and dragged off to the headmaster's office, protesting his innocence. As far as I was concerned Craig deserved what he got for swapping in the first place.

Now I had the tooth back I could relax a little, and was soon involved in a game of tag, and not long later, as happened in all my games of tag, I went down in a heap with four or five others. I was wrestling away happily on the floor, for a full five minutes, before I remembered the tooth in my trouser pocket. Ooops! I stood up, and gingerly removed four pieces of a tooth that had survived intact for 50 million years.

Yours confessingly,

Andrew

Warwickshire

Dear Simon,

After many years of deep shame, I feel compelled to confess a dreadful crime which I committed as a youth some twenty years ago against a purveyor of knowledge in my local learning establishment. It took place in the United States, but my guilt is so strong that I can no longer turn away.

I was twelve years old, and living in a very small Midwestern town. Although I was a decent student, the bane of my life (and of the entire school for that matter) was a teacher named Mr Pearce. He was a dreadful man, about a trillion years old, stone deaf, half blind, and in the throes of advanced madness. He regularly marked students down for not attending classes when they were actually there – he just couldn't see or hear them. His grading system worked purely on the principle that whoever could be the biggest bootlicker got the best grades. On one occasion Mr Pearce gave the entire class (myself included) an assignment to complete, an essay on American Government in the 1800s, and the class duly turned in the assignment one week later. The next day we were shocked to learn that he had failed all of us, saying that we had all written about the wrong subject! He claimed that the assignment was on the Spanish-American War. This was too much to take – we protested to the school authorities. How could thirty-four people all be wrong and just one (Mr Pearce) be right? Our protests were to be in vain, however, as they knew what a nasty man Mr Pearce was, and tackling him over the issue was more than their jobs were worth. All of us then had to explain to our parents why we had failed – needless to say they found the explanations hard to believe and we suffered various forms of purgatory. I vowed then and there that ultimate vengeance would be mine.

It was about this time that an advertisement was appearing on television for the Volkswagen Beetle. Since Mr Pearce drove one, I had grown to hate them (and still do for that matter). In the commercial, a man demonstrated how well assembled they were by driving one into a lake, and showing that it floated. I would have dearly loved to have done this with Mr Pearce's car, but I was too short to even reach the pedals, and there was no way that I was going to steal a car anyway. And that's when it dawned on me – if Volkswagen Beetles were so well assembled that they floated because they wouldn't let water leak in . . .

That night I went round to Mr Pearce's house with my trusty screwdriver and forced the window of his Beetle down a few inches. Working quickly, I grabbed the garden hose from in front of his house, placed the nozzle through the window and turned on the water full blast. Thirty nervous minutes later the deed was done – the car completely filled with water, frame resting on the ground. And it worked! It didn't leak out at all! I decided to complete the effect – I ran home, took two of my pet goldfish from their tank, ran back and put them through the window and into the car. It was clear that they loved their huge new home, and it was a remarkable sight to behold.

The next day at school was one I will never forget. Late morning, the entire school was called into the assembly hall for an announcement. Mr Pearce was in hospital! Overnight, someone had filled his car with water, and when he attempted to evacuate the water by opening the door, he was knocked down by a Beetle-size wave, hit his head on the pavement and had been knocked unconscious! I felt sick – but when they said he should recover in a few days, this changed to total satisfaction. This event proved to be the final straw in his teaching career – Mr Pearce never came back, taking retirement on grounds of nervous exhaustion. This might well have been influenced by the fact that the incident was extensively covered in the local newspaper (front page, no less) under the headline 'Teacher's Teutonic Tidal Wave Terror'.

I don't want Mr Pearce's forgiveness, as the old misery richly deserved his soaking, but seek absolution from goldfish lovers everywhere for bringing the lives of two scaly surfers to a premature if somewhat spectacular end. Forgiven?

Fishing for forgiveness,
Awash With Regrets.

P.S. Although his car was fixed (eventually), he was on a water meter and ended up paying for the hundreds of gallons used in the process. Am I still forgiven?

South Devon

Dear Simon,

During the early seventies I attended a local mixed Grammar School and it is here that the tale unfolds. One very wet and windy afternoon our double games lesson was transferred indoors (basically because the teachers were wimps) and the class was divided in two. This was because there were about sixty of us and we wouldn't all fit in the gym.

My half was seconded to the main hall to play table tennis on two ancient tables; one on the stage and one on the floor of the hall.

It was during the inevitable wait for a game that I noticed a large, obviously new, black fire extinguisher fixed to the wall in one of the stage wings. It was the CO_2 type, you know, the ones with the big nozzle to aim the gas.

Having a ping pong ball in hand I absent-mindedly wondered if the ball would fit into the nozzle (as you do). It did.

I then discovered that I couldn't retrieve it, and indeed my efforts to do so only succeeded in jamming it further down. I decided to abandon the scene completely for fear of ridicule from the teacher and quietly rejoined the queue for a game. As you can imagine it wasn't long before I had forgotten the incident completely.

Two weeks later. 8.45 am Assembly.

Centre stage: large metal box flanked by our Headmaster and a fireman in full firefighting kit, complete with large black fire extinguisher.

The Head explained that because the school had been fitted out with new extinguishers, there would now be a demonstration of their use and application by a member of the Devon Fire Brigade. Everyone was fascinated, including me, although mine was due to impending doom more than anything else.

The fireman then produced a large container of methylated spirits, most of which he emptied onto rags in the metal box. He then tossed in a lighted match and stood back with the Headmaster to wait for the fire to reach a suitable height.

What happened next was like something out of a Tom Sharpe

novel. After about three attempts to start the extinguisher, the fireman and the Head were visibly worried about the growing inferno, which was threatening to require more firemen than planned. Alarmed, the fireman shook the extinguisher vigorously and yanked the trigger. This was too much for my ping pong ball which, with Exocet-like speed and accuracy, shot out of the nozzle, ricocheted off the wooden floor of the stage and hit the Headmaster in a vulnerable part of his anatomy!

All hell broke loose. The Head was understandably poleaxed by this unexpected assault and had to be helped from the stage by two colleagues who themselves looked rather apoplectic, either from anger or, more probably, suppressed laughter. This took place amidst clouds of smoke, flame and CO_2 as the fireman eventually got around to putting out the fire. The other three hundred occupants of the hall were laughing uncontrollably, all, that is, except me, as I was contemplating suicide or, at the very least, joining the Foreign Legion.

It took ten minutes to restore order, although everyone present was prone to fits of giggling for a lot longer. I escaped detection, although everyone at the table tennis class was interrogated. It wasn't until over a year later that I owned up to my friends, after the Head had retired.

I therefore seek forgiveness not from the Head, who was a turkey anyway, or from the other pupils who thoroughly enjoyed the event, but from the poor fireman, who must have thought he was in a living nightmare.

Yours in hope,

anon

Bootle

Dear Father Mayo,

This story goes way back into the mists of time (about fifteen years ago) when I was an altar boy.

I had my name down to do a requiem along with two other altar servers – whom we will call Al and Tim. As per the rules, we arrived about half an hour before the mass was about to start and as we were getting ready, Al remarked on a strong pungent odour that was hanging around in the air.

After a lot of searching, we discovered that the smell was originating from the head of Tim. After discussing what we should do, Al and myself did the good and honest thing and beat Tim up so he would tell us what the heinous aroma was. It turned out that the smell was from some nasty substance used to kill head lice that he had to wash his hair with twice a day.

Anyway, Al and I were to be acolytes (the guys who had to carry the candles) and Tim was the thurible bearer (the one who waves the incense burner). The hearse arrived outside the church, so we arranged ourselves in the correct order for the funeral procession. Tim with the thurible at the front, Al and I with the candles and the priest behind us. Now all we had to wait for was the coffin to be carried out of the hearse, and we would make our way down the aisle to escort the coffin and mourners into the church.

The pall bearers seemed to have some trouble, so we were waiting quite a while for the procession to start. As the candle holders were very heavy, the best way to hold them for any amount of time was to rest the base against your hip and hold the candle out about 45° in front of you, so that's what Al and I did. After about four minutes, the pall bearers seemed to get their act together and started moving. Al turned to tell the priest what was happening and we heard a hissing, popping, crackling noise then an instant later a loud woof sound. After turning to see what the noise was we noticed that Al's candle had touched Tim's hair. Not only was the concoction on the hair supposed to kill lice, but seemingly it was also very flammable indeed.

The show must go on, so we started down the aisle with the acolytes laughing so much that they were crying, the thurible bearer's head smoking more than the incense, and a very displeased priest trying his best to read out the text of the mass.

Needless to say, the team of Al, Tim and myself was never asked to serve a requiem again.

I do not seek forgiveness for annoying the priest with our sniggering throughout the mass, but I wish to be forgiven for the way in which we walked towards the mourners with Tim looking like something out of a Tom and Jerry cartoon with Al and I laughing behind him, thus upsetting the poor family even more than they were already.

Thinking back, Al should have patented his method of ridding head infestations. Tim's problem never did return. Neither did his hair – properly!

Yours seeking forgiveness,

Chris

Address withheld

Father Mayo,

About four years ago I used to be an altar server at my local church, St Wilfred's. St Wilfred's being a small Catholic church meant that it was not always full, but the same old people were there every week. It was early one Sunday when I committed the deadly sin. The church used to have two masses. One at nine-thirty and one at eleven, and I used to serve in them both, along with a friend. The priest was always boring and always very strict. My friend and I decided to liven up the mass by substituting the water for gin that I had taken from home.

As you might have guessed, the priest said mass at nine-thirty and drank the gin, he said mass again at eleven and drank the gin. His words were already beginning to sound slurred and his eye and hand co-ordination was not working, as he managed to burn his hand in the candles on the altar.

When mass was over a member of the congregation came over to my friend and me, and asked us if we thought the priest was drunk. I don't know what came over us but we said yes, he was drinking before mass and was over the pub before he came here. We had to go and get him out.

Well, it didn't take long for the word to get around that the priest was drunk when he said mass.

I ask for forgiveness for spiking his drink, telling lies about him and causing the priest much embarrassment and stress.

Yours hoping to be forgiven,

Bramcote Hills
Nottingham

Dear Simon,

This is not actually my confession but the confession of my longtime boyfriend, who will remain unnamed.

When I was about ten years old my sister, brother and I were all members of the local swimming club and every Tuesday evening my mum used to walk with us to the baths. We always went the same way and I would become excited when passing a certain house as it had a large ornamental fishpond in the front garden with a birdbath as a centrepiece. I used to jump over and look over the wall and watch the goldfish in wonder, until one evening when I looked over, the pond had been filled in and made into a rose garden. I was horrified and Tuesday Club nights were never the same again.

Some fifteen years later my boyfriend related one of his fishing tales to me.

When he was about thirteen, he and a friend had been fishing in Wollaton Park lake and he had managed to catch a pike which by all accounts was about five pounds in weight and nearly two foot long. He was understandably very proud of his catch and promptly wrapped it in wet rags, placed it in his fishing basket and struggled home with it.

Pike are hardy creatures and upon reaching home he filled the bath and placed his prize specimen therein for his mother's approval. His mum was not happy with the new tenant of her bath and insisted that the following day he should get rid of it. Bearing in mind that this fish was his pride and joy he and a friend struck on a solution. They placed the pike in a carrier bag and when the dark of the evening arrived they took it to its new home – a large ornamental fishpond of a house on the way to the swimming baths.

When this story was told to me I immediately made the connection with the pond I used to love and look at as a child and quickly realized the grisly truth.

I would therefore like to apologize on my boyfriend's behalf to the owners of that fishpond and the goldfish within, as I cannot imagine their horror to find a five-pound pike (which no doubt was heavier after its diet of goldfish) in the pond.

This all happened some twenty-odd years ago and I would like to think that the sin can now be forgiven.

Ann

Ash Hill

Dear Simon,

As a student of the local college – some years ago – money was short, so to supplement one's drinking habits a part-time job was required. Now due to the large number of students, jobs were in short supply, so it was to my Gran I turned for inspiration. Dog walking was the idea she came up with – pointing out that from her group of friends, I had a ready-made client bank.

The idea was that I'd walk the dogs twice a day, for half an hour, three times a week, for a nominal fee. Everyone was happy and all went smoothly for two weeks, but as with many jobs the boredom set in. Same dogs, same route and it was starting to take its toll on my legs and patience.,

Then an idea struck me. Shorter, faster walks would have better results. The dogs would be fitter – and I'd have more time to myself – yet I'd still earn the dough. With this in mind I took to taking the dogs for a walk alongside me as I cycled. I could go at some speed and the dogs managed to keep up – well, almost!

Now at this stage I must point out that my grandmother is aged 79 and as her friends are of around the same age, the dogs are no spring chickens either. So as I look back now – I realize the error of my ways.

Duke, a lovely Irish setter who loved a run, was the first to go. At least that was how it seemed. He followed the bike, his tongue hanging out – happily lolloping behind – or maybe his tongue was hanging out because I was pedalling at around 40 miles an hour. Poor Duke limped home, and when I went to call for him the next day he refused to budge. His owner was bewildered – Duke had always liked a walk – but just put his subsequent rheumatism down to old age.

The much faster and much shorter walks started to take their toll. I had four dogs down in the space of three weeks, but I'd made my money so it was time to call it a day before any more dodgy doggy dilemmas occurred.

Only one owner insisted I couldn't let her down. Her labrador, Penny, needed a walk – I couldn't mess people around this way. All right, Penny would get her run – boy, did she run! 'Was it a bird? Was it a plane?' No, it was Penny the Labrador. Like a streak of lightning, feet barely touching the ground as she hurtled along behind my bike. She went home exhausted but I didn't care as I was never going to call on her owner again.

Being a loving grandson, I called at Granny's house the next day to be faced with the news. Penny the unlucky labrador had died in the night! Granny said she knew why I was so distressed 'Yes – it's so easy to get attached to a lovely dog like that but the vet said old age catches up with all of us eventually!!'

Well, I'd got away with it – but ever since my heart has been heavy. Now I'm not a man to argue with a professional's opinion – the vet obviously knows more about animals than I do – but just in case – Simon, am I forgiven?

Anonymous

Beaconsfield

Dear Father Simon,

Forgive me as I have sinned. It was twenty years ago when I was a chorister and our parish church had a coffee morning and jumble sale to raise funds for one of the church appendages . . . the spire.

The coffee morning was a roaring success, and raised the princely sum of eleven quid. However there were several items left unsold, one of which was a tailor's dummy. The problem was what to do with it and the other items left over. Eventually they were all bundled into a storeroom along with the broken chairs and ping pong tables that most churches seem to collect.

It was whilst in the storeroom that my fellow conspirators and I hatched our plan. With someone keeping lookout the dummy's arms were detached just above the elbow as I remember. Then it was off to the graveyard.

Once again lookouts were posted and a suitable grave found. The arms were then planted just down from the headstone and we all retired to the bushes to await results. I would like to apologise to the old lady who tended the graves, and the guests of a wedding who had started to arrive. As their cries of horror reached us we scarpered.

The happy couple whose wedding it was probably wondered why the trebles collapsed with laughter when the vicar said 'they should join their hands together in holy matrimony'.

Still, it was all harmless fun really.

Yours faithfully,

Keep It in the Family

Politician fights politician, party fights party, country fights country. Surely mankind is capable of many dark deeds. But few so dark as those we are prepared to commit against our oldest enemy – other members of our own family. If the United Nations had an inter-family peace-keeping force, on the evidence of this chapter, it would be exceedingly busy.

Dear Father Simon,

I have a confession to make which is so shameful I have not got the courage to give you my name.

One lazy family Sunday afternoon, my eldest brother got out his recent family holiday snaps. Being very bored, I flicked through them quickly. I was intrigued to find that only seventeen photographs had come out, so I studied the negatives to find out what had gone wrong.

Imagine my surprise when I realized all twenty-four photographs had in fact come out, but seven had been removed from the batch! These photographs were of my brother's wife in various states of undress. I slyly pocketed these negatives, and handed the holiday snaps back to my brother.

The next day, I nipped down to the chemist and had some copies of the saucy photos made up. I then sent them off to one of those naughty national magazines, entering them in the 'Readers' Wives' section.

Well, several weeks passed before I was summoned to a family conference along with my two other brothers. Father interrogated us three while our eldest brother looked on. In one hand he held a copy of the magazine in which his wife appeared as 'Julie from Newcastle' – and in his other hand he held a cheque from the magazine for £50.00 for the use of the photographs.

I managed to plead my innocence and finally one of my other brothers was accused.

I hope both of my brothers can forgive me although I dare not let them know.

Yours,

Anon

Abbots Langley
Herts

Dear Simon,

My confession goes back to 1988 when our son Matthew was five years old. Along with one son, we also had three golden retrievers, Pasha, Cassie and Amber, one cat, T.C., and one hamster, Sparkie.

The day is Christmas Eve, the house is bedlam, one very excited five-year-old is waiting for Father Christmas. We finally got Matthew to bed and asleep, then set about getting out the presents that 'Father Christmas' had brought. At last everything was ready and Derek and I went to bed, only to be woken by one of our dogs, Cassie, crying. I found her in another bedroom. I just patted her and told her Father Christmas wouldn't be long and went back to bed. We heard nothing more until Matthew woke up. Great excitement, the living-room was a bomb site within fifteen minutes. Then horror, where was the hamster, he wasn't in his cage. 'Let's all look for Sparkie,' I said, so off we went.

I went into the bedroom where Cassie had been the night before and found poor Sparkie dead on the floor. Cassie must have had him in her mouth when I went in to her the night before. He must have got out of his cage and Cassie must have thought Father Christmas had come early and taken him upstairs to play with him, only she killed him instead.

I told Derek and we had to dispose of poor Sparkie before Matthew caught on. Matthew couldn't find Sparkie anywhere, so we told him that he must have gone off with Father Christmas in his sack. Matthew, being only five, seemed to believe us.

He still asks about what happened to Sparkie. How could we tell him the truth, he would hate Cassie for killing him. Sadly, Cassie is no longer with us, but remains in our thoughts, especially over Christmas, the time of year when Sparkie went to play with 'Father Christmas'.

I hope we can be forgiven for lying to our five-year-old son, but how could we have told him that the dog had killed his hamster on Christmas Eve?

Would you tell your son the truth?

Merry Christmas,
Love,
Tina

P.S. One day I will confess all about one of our other dogs and Matthew's gold chain!

Co Durham

Dear Simon,

In January 1979 I was seven months pregnant with my second daughter. It was snowing heavily. At 7.20 p.m. I had put my three-year-old to bed when my husband came in from work with the flu.

As you know, Simon, men seem to get the flu a lot worse than women. He lay on the sofa and asked me with pleading eyes to go to our local corner shop, which is about 600 yards away, to buy him some LemSip, which I did.

The snow got worse. He then asked me to go back to the shop to buy him a miniature bottle of whisky. This I did.

The next time it was for a bottle of lemonade.

At seven months pregnant, in the snow, I'd had enough, so I gave him three small pills and told him that the little old lady who owned the shop said that they were a miracle cure for the flu.

He took them and the next morning said he felt a lot better and went to work.

He has never known that the pills I gave him were contraceptive pills. (Well, I didn't need them, did I?)

I beg forgiveness for lying to my husband, but especially for saying that the little old lady in the corner shop had given me them. I can't ask her forgiveness because she's dead now.

Anon.

Dear Father Mayo,

On behalf of my mother I wish to offload the guilt of a secret held in the family closet since the perfect family Christmas of 1979 when a lively bottle of tonic water nearly brought disaster to the household.

Picture the perfect family Christmas scene with Mother, Father, brother, Gran and Great Gran, eighty-two years of age and marginally senile, sitting around watching the Queen or anything else served up by the television companies after a thorough stuffing of turkey.

In an attempt to enliven the proceedings, Mother, well known in the family for not being quite the full shilling, offered drinks to the family. For reasons known only to herself, Great Gran requested a whisky and tonic water and duly received a large tumbler containing a triple whisky diluted to the top with tonic water. With dainty eighty-two-year-old elegance this was downed and about twenty minutes later a further tumbler of tonic requested in order that she might take her heart pills.

After taking two tablets with the tumbler of tonic, I noticed with amusement that the old bird was slurring her words slightly. Mild amusement changed to marked interest when she started to slump in her chair. The slump then deepened into a deep, deep sleep. It was only when she failed to be roused by prodding, loud talking, slapping around the face and other strenuous attempts to wake her that we decided something was obviously very wrong. An ambulance was called.

In the short time between the ambulance being dispatched and arriving the cold realization dawned. One week previously, Mother and Father had attended a party. The bringing of a bottle had been requested but being cheap they had bought a bottle of vodka and decanted half into the only available receptacle before proceeding to the party armed with a half-full bottle of vodka. Of course, the only available receptacle had been an empty tonic water bottle which had then assumed the identity of a full bottle of rather flat tonic water. Mother had given her gran two full tumblers of vodka only slightly diluted by a triple whisky. The downing of just under half a bottle of vodka in just under half an hour was now obvious as the cause of her slumbers. In addition, she had taken two heart tablets.

The ambulance duly arrived, its aerial bedecked with Christmas tinsel and condoms, the paramedics equally as festive and the drunken biddy wheeled away to hospital to be examined. There were many curtains twitching in the quiet cul-de-sac as the ambulance departed.

At hospital, she was, not surprisingly, pronounced very drunk but otherwise OK and the heart pills identified as diuretics. By this time Great Gran was beginning to get a little frisky. Never ever drunk in her life before, the alcohol was having strange effects on her brain's inhibitory centres. Doctors were propositioned and flashed at as they passed this normally quiet and demure eighty-two-year-old lady. Once reasonably sober, she was sent home to sleep it off and we were sent away.

Expecting a very groggy hung-over Granny the following morning Mother was surprised to be woken at 6.30 am Boxing Day by the sound of Gran washing pots with fabric conditioner, completely oblivious to the previous day's events.

Father Mayo, I seek forgiveness for Mother, whose attempt to enliven the usual boring family Christmas resulted in one never to be forgotten. Please forgive her, not for the Granny whose taste buds couldn't tell the difference between tonic water and neat vodka, who didn't even suffer with a hang-over and who, to her dying day, never knew why she managed to miss the James Bond film. Father Mayo, I seek forgiveness on behalf of Mother from the ambulance and hospital staff who had to deal with this mini crisis on Christmas Day and who were quite marvellous and patient. Perhaps a reminder of those who have to work to care for others over the festive season.

Purton
Wiltshire

Dear Simon,

I just had to write to you after your Confessions prompted my brother, Mark, to confess all, thereby solving one of life's mysteries!

To explain: the story starts in 1981, when I had just purchased a brand new Honda 90 motorbike. After only three months, the bike continually broke down, resulting in many heated rows with the supplier – who reluctantly had to provide a full refund.

No more thought was given to the problem until recently, when my brother, Mark, confessed that, while I was asleep after a night shift, he'd taken the motorbike for a scrambling session with some friends along the canal bank. Yes – you've guessed it – the motorbike ended up in the canal, which damaged all the electrics. This explains the constant breakdowns.

So your confessions spot has cleared up that little mystery. Not that it has made much difference to my relationship with my now deceased (only joking) brother.

COLIN

Drayton
Norwich

Dear Father Simon,

Family Confessions? You won't get one better than this!

Having for many years been aware of this hideous misdemeanour, I feel that it is now time to grovel at your feet (very apt in this case) to humbly beg forgiveness – mainly for the concealment of the act in question.

The dirty deed in fact had 'nothing' to do with my sweet self but primarily my sisters who I feel require the greatest redemption. They have always taken pleasure in playing practical jokes – particularly on our father.

About ten years ago my oldest sister purchased an implement for reducing the hard skin on the bottom of the feet. I'm sure you know the sort of thing, it looked and worked something like a cheese-grater and my three sisters who shared a flat at the time spent many happy hours collecting the grisly shavings from their non-too-savoury feet.

These they put into a Parmesan cheese container and when it was suffi-ciently full posted it to my father who, not being stupid, did not touch it with a bargepole. However, my brother coming home from work in desperate need of nourishment made himself some pasta. He thought his luck was in and that my mother, who is strictly a Cheddar lady, had been possessed by an unusual fit of generosity while last out shopping. He sprinkled it liberally on his meal and scoffed the lot.

It is for the knowledge of this crime that I beg my pardon; for the fact that not only does my brother not know the truth to this day but also that he is vegetarian and has partaken of not only animal, but human flesh (albeit waste product!)

I rest my case.

Yours seeking absolution,

63

Norwich

Simon,

Bless me father, for I have sinned . . . I have to confess to something I did over Christmas.

For ages my mother had been nagging my father about all the old cine films that he has accumulated over the past 30-odd years – clips of their wedding, *all* my sisters' and my birthday parties, our family, friends and pets too!

Almost anything any of us did he would have to film it. The films were in such a mess that Dad decided, as a Christmas surprise for Mum, to have them all transferred on to VHS video cassettes. Twenty-odd messy tapes soon condensed down into two neat modern ones. Great!

Christmas Eve, my father gathered Mum, my sister and me into the lounge to watch him throw all the old tapes onto the big open fire. Mum went into a state of shock, while all Dad could do was smile and say 'Wait until tomorrow'!

Christmas Day arrived and my mother was over the moon (and relieved) with her present. But, with this being a rather busy time of year with plenty of good films on TV, we never got round to watching them.

It wasn't until January that I decided to watch a few things I had videoed over the festive season. First of all I put on the film *Dirty Dancing* followed by several clips of 'Top of the Pops'. Then, to my horror, I noticed a rather familiar face on the screen. It was my 28-year-old sister celebrating her fifth birthday. This only lasted a few seconds then the tape ended.

I felt sick. I scrambled about, praying the second 'Family Memories' tape was still OK.

As I pushed it into the machine and pressed 'play', the same 'I might as well just kill myself now' feeling filled my body, as Henry and Madge Ramsey came up on the screen, followed by the TV show 'Blind Date', and other rather important things of equal interest. Thirty years of family history gone!!

My parents have not yet discovered what's happened. If it's any consolation . . . Mum and Dad, you are better dancers than Patrick Swayze and Jennifer Grey, and big sis, you look better with your clothes on and no potty on your head!

Am I forgiven?

Elisha

Sussex

Dear Simon,

This confession makes me shake every time I think of it. I hope you can forgive me. It goes back to a festive season of my youth. We didn't get our usual Christmas presents from Uncle Eric and Auntie Sheila in Australia, but then a mysterious pot of exotic-smelling herbs and spices arrived from Oz. Mum put them in the Christmas pud and it tasted great. We ate half and kept the rest in the fridge.

A week later we heard from Auntie Sheila that Uncle Eric had died and had we received his ashes to bury in Britain?

Fortunately our father is a minister so we were able to have a little service of internment for the remainder of the pudding, or should that be the remains of Uncle Eric?

We are really sorry; we wouldn't have eaten Uncle Eric if we'd known. Can we be forgiven?

THE WILKINSONS

Nottingham

Dear Darling Twiglet-legs,

HELP! I have a dark and murky secret lurking in my dim and distant past, and I badly need to repent. if I do not unburden my soul soon, then I shall be driven completely around the twist by the suspense of wondering what my family's reactions will be when they finally discover the hidden skeleton in my cupboard . . .

It happened ten years ago, in the summer holidays, when I was nine. My mum, my sister and I all went off to stay with my nan, and as luck would have it, my nan's sister was also staying there – Great Auntie Elsie (GAE). You know what it's like when you're little: you go out shopping and end up spending half the day hanging about in the street because some ancient old lady stops to talk to you. Even if you think you've never seen her before, she raves on about how cute you used to look sitting in your pram sucking a dummy!

Anyway, on this particular occasion I was really fed up. The entire day had been wasted and we only had enough time to go into one more shop before they all shut. GAE wanted to treat herself to a new pair of drawers – we are not talking normal simple drawers here, we are talking megaknickers – the ever-so-gorgeous woolly sort which reach down to your knees! Well, after ages deciding which ones to buy, we eventually went home.

Later on that evening, when everybody was watching TV, I just happened to be passing GAE's bedroom, and what do you think were sitting on the bed still in a brown paper bag? Yes! You've guessed! Such a delicate shade of peach, the white frilly lace was very fetching, so attractive, so alluring, so . . .

I had a nice new biro in my hand, and suddenly I was taken by some mysterious force. Before I knew what was happening I had written a very appropriate message on the left cheek – 'I ♥ SEX'!! I don't know what came over me, honestly!!

Well, as you can imagine, there were fireworks when my artistic graf-

66

fito was discovered. Luckily, while we were all rolling around on the floor with laughter (apart from the unlucky victim, who was screeching, 'I'm disgusted, it's an outrage!'), nobody noticed the twinkling in my innocent eyes. The next day we marched back to the shop and demanded to see the manager, who promised to interrogate all the staff. It was eventually deduced that the Saturday girl had gone a bit wild when pricing the delightful garment, so she was promptly sent off to price knickers in the job centre!

To this day no one suspects me in the slightest, but I feel that the time has come to confess. Perhaps I will now be able to get dressed in the morning without smirking! I only hope that GAE is not listening, or I'm likely to be exiled to some remote part of the globe!

Am I forgiven?

Yours faithfully,

A poor student, who you may call Dummy!

Leamington Spa

Dear Simon,

I wish to confess to you all about my Boxing Day prank in 1989.

It concerns my five-year-old son (who is now eight years old and completely recovered from his ordeal), and his grandfather (my dad).

I was separated from my wife and living at home with my parents at the time. My four children were spending Boxing Day with me.

I had bought David (my son) a radio-controlled tank as his present. It was a beaut. 360° turret, with 0.5 mm gun, machine guns, missiles, three forward and one reverse gears, and video-screen targetting. (Saddam would love a fleet of these.)

We had our lunch and numerous drinks, and we all retired to the lounge to watch the afternoon film. My father slept on the sofa face down.

Bored with the film I decided to give my son's tank a test drive. I sent it round the room, over the dog's ears and knocked over various drinks on my front room 'recce' operation. I realized then that the tank was about five feet from my father at about 90° to the side of his head.

I switched on the video viewfinder, armed the guns, and lowered the main gun turret until I had my father's left ear in my sights. With an evil grin I pressed the 'fire' button. The tank then launched a 0.5 mm earwax-piercing shell, smack, straight in his lughole. Perfect shot.

My father jerked about two feet off the sofa, still horizontal.

I quickly replaced the handset in my son's hands.

You may guess the rest; my father jumped up, snatched the tank off David shouting and snarling, 'I'm putting this away and you can go and sit upstairs until tea-time!'

David, protesting his innocence, and doing a good job of trying to grass me up, was dragged upstairs kicking and screaming. My father returned five minutes later saying things like, 'Those tanks are b——— lethal in the hands of children.' I sat and said nothing.

Can you forgive me? My son still tells his grandfather 'It was Daddy.'

Ian

And am I covered by the Geneva war convention?

Newport
Gwent

Dear Simon,

I'm afraid I can't reveal my full name, since it could cost me dear. This confession goes back to last summer, when my father had a new computer system fitted in his offices.

One Friday lunchtime, my mother asked me to drive to the office because Dad had phoned to say he'd left his wallet at home. I drove over but found that the office door was locked. Luckily, I had a key and I went upstairs. The office was deserted. Maybe the office computer would explain where everyone was.

I turned on a monitor and pressed a few keys. Nothing seemed to happen. I played around for a few minutes, when suddenly a message appeared on the screen. It said 'Abort, Yes/No?' I typed 'Yes' and the screen went blank. I got up hurriedly and turning off the monitor, I turned to leave. As I left, I noticed a sign on the back of the door which said, 'Gone for lunch at Terry's'.

I soon found out that all the office staff were out to lunch to celebrate the completion of the computer system and its connection to the computer systems of ten other branches of the firm. I gave Dad the wallet and left.

That evening, Dad came home in a huge temper. Apparently someone in his branch had wiped out the whole computer file – not just in his branch, but in another six branches around the country as well. The cost for all the repairs would be almost £4,000.

Needless to say, I've kept quiet for some months but feel that I can confess now. I hope I have your forgiveness!

Yours beggingly,

David

Hemel Hempstead
Herts

Dear Simon,

This story goes back four years, when I went to visit my mum and dad who live near the coast.

It was a Saturday morning and my mum suggested we go shopping and whilst we were in the town centre she said she wanted to change a kettle she had bought. A simple enough task I thought, so we went into the shop. My then girlfriend and I were browsing at foodblenders and TVs, like you do. My mum was talking to a salesman, trying to exchange the kettle.

It was all quiet in the shop when suddenly we could hear voices being raised. The salesman was talking to my mum in a rather loud voice by now and people were starting to turn around and watch. The voices got louder and louder, by now they were shouting at each other. I suddenly flipped. I couldn't stand back and let this man shout at my mum, so I went over to him, grabbed him by the lapels and said, 'Right, outside!' To my horror he said, 'OK then.' We went outside and carried on shouting at each other. My mum and then girlfriend were really embarrassed by now and just wanted to go home.

The crowds had gathered and at this stage we were pushing and shoving each other. Suddenly the manager of the store came out and diffused the situation. He had a new kettle in his hands and gave it to my mum and apologized, he also gave her some vouchers to spend in the shop.

The crowd dispersed and we walked away. I was quite proud of myself for sticking up for my mum and thought justice had been done. I could see by my mum's face that something was wrong. 'What's wrong'? I said. 'You're entitled to change a kettle if it doesn't work'. 'I know,' she said, 'but I didn't buy it from there, I got it from the local market.' I stopped in my tracks, I couldn't believe what I had just done.

To make things even worse my dad found out that the salesman had been sacked on the Monday morning for being rude to a customer!

So please forgive me for grabbing the salesman by the lapels and shouting at him, and my mum for telling a little porkie!!

Tony

Don't Tell the
Animal Liberation Front

You have to believe me, I am, I really am, an animal lover. Dogs, hamsters, horses, goats. You name it, I'll stroke it. It's just that this is my favourite chapter, full of really dreadful stories which have all in their time kept many a poor BBC duty officer very, very busy.

Whitminster
Gloucestershire

Dear Father Simon,

To say that this confession has played on my mind for some years would be to tell a monster lie. I have to take you back to 1976. My family were living in Weymouth at the time and I was on a weekend visit. Also down for the weekend was my brother Simon. Now anyone who remembers the mid 70s will know that if Tom and Jerry were on television everything else stopped. In this particular cartoon Tom was pushed through a letter box by Spike, that big bulldog character who often turned up. 'What a good idea!' I exclaimed. 'Must try that.' So Simon and I left the lounge and headed for the front door. After several minutes of effort Simon and I had to admit defeat. With sheepish looks on our faces we had to ask for help.

Let me point out that no harm came to any animal, unless you count long-suffering parents as part of the animal kingdom. The sight that met my mother's eyes was enough to give a heart attack to anyone. Jammed into the letter box was a mass of ginger fur, not unlike Mum's beloved cat, Oedipus.

As you can imagine the next few seconds were bedlam. An angry mum is a very aggressive animal.

After tempers cooled and two thick ears were attended to, all was eventually forgiven.

I don't ask absolution for Simon or myself as I still think it's very funny. I don't seek it from our mother as, like all mothers, they have to put up with that type of prank. But it's from my dad that I seek forgiveness. At the time he had a painful back. The sight of the cat in the letter box put his recovery back several weeks. No parents should have to suffer that type of abuse.

Please send your absolution to my brother and myself. I throw ourselves on your mercy.

Yours sincerely,

Tony

P.S. Actually we used a fur hat that just looked like our cat!

73

Towcester
Northants

Dear Simon,

This confession is aimed at an unknown Cornish farmer (we didn't stay long enough to find out his name) who lets a field out to campers.

Four of us, Brett, Russell, Steve and I, pitched our tent in his field one Friday, shortly before opening time.

Well, at about eleven o'clock, they poured us out of the village inn, and we were wobbling back up the moonlit lane, when Steve thought he'd sussed out a short cut across the fields. Walking anywhere wasn't easy by then, but we climbed over the gate and set out across the grass.

Cornwall has got loads of abandoned tin mines and we'd only gone a little way when we stumbled into a flimsy fence around a very big black hole. The fields were dotted with open shafts and this one was a particularly large one.

Then someone had the bright idea of seeing how deep it was. So we tossed a stone in and listened for the sound. Nothing. So then a rock gets lobbed in. Again not a sound. So then Steve and I levered a boulder out of the ground and manhandled it over the edge. Again, not a peep.

We were determined to find out how deep it was, but there isn't a lot lying around in your average field that's going to make a lot of noise. Then Brett and Russell discovered a railway sleeper and tossed that into the void. So we're all craning forward around the edge for some sound when suddenly this chain comes snaking through the grass between us, and a goat with a clump of grass in its mouth goes flying straight past us into the hole!!

Obviously the farmer tethered the goat to the sleeper to stop it wandering down one of the shafts, but he hadn't banked on the sleeper going in first. The goat didn't even get a chance to bleat.

That sobered us right up and we left early the next day – for Devon. No mines there!

Yours guiltily,

Colin

P.S. I don't think you'll want to broadcast this one but it might make you chuckle.

A builder friend of mine ran over a cat in his truck, stopped to see if it had survived and found it lying on the pavement, but still breathing. So he got out a spade from the truck, belted it over the head to put it out of its misery and went on his way feeling remorseful.

Two days later there was a knock at the door and a policeman stood there asking if it was his truck parked outside.

Apparently they had received a complaint from some old dear who was watching from her front window as her kitty had a snooze when some lunatic came up, clouted her cat over the head and threw it into the hedge.

The cat he actually ran over was still wedged in the wheel arch of the truck.

                                                        Crewe
                                                        Cheshire

Dear Simon,

I grew up in the North Staffordshire countryside. Unfortunately for reasons I won't bore you with I had to move to a town about fifteen miles away. I still kept in touch with a good friend of mine called Paul, and occasionally we'd visit each other. This confession dates from 1990 when we were twenty and had just discovered the delights of clay pigeon shooting. I would drive to his house, we'd pack the equipment in the back of the car and then we'd drive off to find a farmer who'd let us use his land. Most of them were very friendly, almost always allowing us to use one of their fields. We usually had to perform some small favour in exchange. This usually involved taking out a few crows instead of clay pigeons.

Unfortunately, neither of the two farmers who usually let us use their land was able to on this particular Saturday afternoon, so we went slightly further afield.

We'd once visited a farmer by the name of Johnston and remembering him to be a friendly old chap, we decided that he'd be worth a try. I was elected spokesman. After parking the car at the front of the house I knocked on his door. Eventually he answered, and after I explained what we wanted he asked me in. He explained that his horse was very ill, and needed putting down. He didn't want to pay for a vet, and he couldn't face doing it himself. He said he'd let us use his land if I shot his horse. He just gave me the directions to the stables at the back.

As I opened the door I saw Paul leaning on the bonnet of the car with his broken rifle cradled in his right arm. He looked so relaxed I decided to shake him up a bit.

I stalked over to the car, snatched up my rifle, loaded it and walked purposefully in the direction of the stables. 'What's up, Ian?' Paul asked jumping to his feet.

'The unreasonable elderly gent has denied us permission to use his land,' I replied (although not using those words). Paul followed me. Once we reached the stables I instantly saw the sickly looking grey, and walked over to it.

'I know,' I said, 'Let's teach him a lesson. Let's shoot his horse.'

With that I shot the poor beast. It was quick, clean and painless. Paul's face was a picture of horror. Suddenly, before I had a chance to explain, or even laugh at his expression, that expression changed to something very unpleasant.

'Yeah!' he shouted, 'Let's kill his bull as well!'

Before I could stop him, he spun round and shot the bull, who was looking over his door to see what was going on. There was a vaguely bovine moan followed by the sound of several tonnes of prime beef hitting the floor of a stable.

There was only one course of action to follow: run, very quickly. We dived into the car and sped off.

Once safely back home I told Paul what had really happened. After he'd calmed down we decided to become ex-clay pigeon shooters.

We'd just like to apologise to Mr Johnston for murdering his bull, and hope both he and you can find it in your hearts to forgive us.

York

Dear Simon,

You've heard of Smokey and the Bandit, haven't you? Well, my confession is called Smokey and the Tunnel.

Smokey was my friend Brian's beautiful and arrogant grey cat. The tunnel was a heavy wooden one through which Brian's Hornby train would run. On rainy afternoons we would play with it, but Smokey was not welcome to join us, as he had so many times before pounced on the train as it sped past him, causing the most awful crashes.

On this particular day, Mallard was pulling all of the eleven trucks that Brian possessed, when in strolled Smokey. Knowing Smokey's past form for creating railway disasters, I brought the train to a halt, so that Brian could remove his marauding moggie.

To save the guard from a severe headache under Smokey's paws, I pulled the train just inside the tunnel. Smokey tensed, his eyes opened wide and he snuck forward, his chin on the deck, until his nose was just inside the tunnel mouth. I made the train move a little more, and as the brake van disappeared into the gloomy depths of the tunnel, Smokey tried to follow it, until the whole of his noble head filled the opening and his sleek stomach was laid upon the Up Main Line. Then I made the train crawl off slowly to see if he would try to struggle after it. Smokey, however, remained unmoved, still staring into the inky blackness, oblivious of the fact that all of the train was now out of the tunnel and moving slowly down the back straight.

Brian and I looked at each other, our minds working as one, but MY hand was on the controller.

I spun it round until it was hard against the stop, and all twelve of Mr Hornby's very best volts galvanized Mallard into action. Wheels spinning, scrabbling for grip like Nigel Mansell launching his Williams Renault from pole position, she hurled her heavy train around the long bend, and when she reached the straight leading to the tunnel, her connecting rods a blur, she was the perfect reincarnation of the REAL Mallard pounding down

Stoke Bank to take the World Speed Record for Britain all those years ago.

Doubtless remembering all the times Smokey had abused her in the past, I swear that she was still gaining speed when she struck that wicked pussie's posterior, and as she did so, several things seemed to happen at once.

Mallard stopped, very suddenly, the rest of her train crashing in a heap around her, and the red button on the controller went 'plop'.

More startling by far was the effect on Smokey. Nothing in his evil life so far had prepared him for being unexpectedly walloped in his posterior parts by a fast and heavy express train. Not only did he let out a banshee wail that echoed through the tunnel, but he also shot about a foot and a half straight upwards. I swear he'd have nearly made the ceiling, but he was hampered by several pounds of tunnel around his neck, which of course went up in the air with him.

A moment later, through our helpless tears of laughter, we could just glimpse a grey furry streak bolt for the bedroom door. Smokey never EVER came to play trains with us again.

Simon, I crave your forgiveness after all these years, not for giving Smokey his comeuppance, which of course he richly deserved, but for misusing such a magnificent model locomotive.

Am I forgiven?

Felmersham
Bedford

Dear Simon,

I've been meaning to get the following off my chest for several years and have decided that having reached the ripe old age of thirty, now would be a good time.

It involves one fourteen-year-old girl, namely me, two goats and a large fuchsia pot plant.

About one week before the incident happened, my mother had brought a large fuchsia plant from our local agricultural show. It was a wonderful specimen and took pride of place on the coffee table in our lounge.

Well about one week later on a bright summer's day, I decided to let my two goats, Heidi and Milly, into our orchard for a romp around. They seemed very grateful at having been let off their tethers and were having a wonderful time eating everything in sight. Feeling quite pleased with myself I left them to it.

About half an hour later I decided to go and see how they were getting on. Into the orchard I went, only to find no goats. I couldn't under-stand where they could have gone. Turning round I saw that the French doors leading into the lounge were wide open. I suddenly felt very sick – there was only one place my goats could be!

I rushed through the French doors to find goat poo all over the carpet, and Heidi and Milly looking at me with mouths full of my mother's fuchsia. I grabbed both goats, wrenched the pieces of fuchsia out of their mouths and dragged them outside, quickly locking them in their shed.

Rushing back inside I swept most of the poo up and then started collecting all the discarded pieces of fuchsia. I gathered them all up and carefully stuck each branch in the soil until it looked as normal as possible. There was nothing much more I could do except wait for my mother's return.

Well, she sat next to the plant all that night and didn't notice anything. I was going mad. Surely she would notice – she always found out when I'd done something.

The next morning she watered her beloved plant. This was followed by a loud shriek. She came rushing into the kitchen clutching what was left of the fuchsia. 'Look at this!' she said, 'I've been done, it's just fallen to bits.' Naturally, I made the necessary noises and said how terrible it was that her wonderful plant had turned out to be a load of rubbish. And that is exactly where it ended up.

Ever since that day, my mother has told the story of the fuchsia that fell to bits.

I hope that somehow you will find it in your heart to forgive me? My mother sold my goats about six months later after they ate her magnolia tree!

Yours with a heavy heart,

81

Dorset

Dear Simon,

This confession goes back to 1964. I was fourteen years old and living near Guildford. The person to whom I must confess is my sister, June, who to this day thinks her pet hamster, Hammy, disappeared by escaping from his cage in our dining room. Wrong.

At this time I was very engrossed in radio-controlled model aircraft and I used to go to a local cricket ground with a friend to fly my latest acquisition, a three-channel 60" wingspan 'KeilKraft Matador'. The actual cricket pitch made a perfectly smooth take-off and landing strip for the aircraft and I soon became very proficient at the controls.

Now there was a television programme called 'Tales of the Riverbank' for younger viewers which featured a hamster which, amongst other things, used to be seen driving a jeep and a boat. So I thought, I wonder if Hammy would like a flight in my aeroplane?

On further discussion with my friend we duly selected a shoe box complete with holes in both ends and transported Hammy and my aeroplane – which had a large cockpit area, plenty of room for Hammy – to the cricket ground. We popped him in, complete with carrots, and, after starting up, taxied him down the runway ready for take-off.

My friend and I lay down on the ground when he went past to get a proper perspective of his size and make the whole flight more realistic. We could see Hammy sitting up looking out through the cockpit window. After three or four circuits of the playing fields I landed him and he was still looking out through the cockpit having obviously enjoyed the whole trip.

This little treat for Hammy was repeated on several more occasions. Until one day, after having taken off, the aeroplane was coming towards us, nice and low for a flypast when I suddenly noticed a distinct slackness in the controls. I made the aircraft turn and bank away in a large arc and on its second flypast I lost radio control altogether. Hammy passed for the last time over our heads, still gazing intently through the front screen, obviously still enjoying himself unaware of the pending disaster.

My continued efforts of frantically prodding the controls for some response were alas to no avail, the aircraft and Hammy continued to climb steadily away into the sunset until it was literally in the clouds and then out of sight. After the shock of losing my aeroplane my thoughts turned to my sister. She adored

Hammy, what was I to do? After some thought I staged a 'breakout' from the hamster cage. That wire is really tough stuff when you try to chomp it with wire cutters to look like it was teeth but, with a little sawdust scattered on the floor, the stage was set.

The final result was very convincing and imagine my relief when my father told my broken-hearted and by now sobbing sister that it was quite common for hamsters to gnaw through wire in this fashion and that Hammy had probably gone out the back door and is now living back with nature.

I'm very sorry and I am glad to have told someone else about the poor hamster's demise.

Yours sincerely,

Keith

Coventry

Dear Saint Simon,

It is time to clear up a mystery that has puzzled our family
for many years. That mystery is: Why did our lovely, happy,
singing budgie suddenly and totally change personality one
day? Many theories have been offered – frightened by the family
cat (nope); frightened by a loud noise (not quite); heart
attack (distinct possibility – read on); or unknown cause? I
can now reveal that the latter is correct. It was, until now,
an unknown cause – me.

It was a fine summer's afternoon. I was eight years old and
on summer break. The only thing on my one-track mind was fun
and games with my friends, who were waiting for me at the park.
First I had to escape from the clutches of the Slave-Driver,
better known as Mum. She had a habit of giving me tasks to
perform just as I was getting ready to go out and play. I was
just about to make my break from my own personal Stalag when I
felt a hand grab my shoulder. Too late – caught by the Head
Screw. 'I'm going out now. I'll be gone for a couple of hours.
Before you go out, make sure you hoover the house from top to
bottom. See you later! And don't forget to clean out the bird
cage!' BANG! went the front door as she left and my plans with
her. I was as infuriated as an eight-year-old can get, which
is pretty infuriated. Great – the whole house! A three-level,
five-bedroom house! Good job she didn't ask me to paint it as
well, I suppose!

Right – if I hurry I can have this done before she returns
and escape from Colditz. I grabbed our trusty chrome canister
vacuum cleaner and starting hoovering like a boy possessed. I
was flying around the house, Simon. If hoovering had been an
Olympic event I would have taken the gold medal. I was
bordering on supersonic when I hit the lounge. As I entered the
room, the noise of Barry the budgie (I didn't name him) singing
happily away in his cage was loud enough to be heard over the
vacuum cleaner, which was no mean feat. Terrific, I thought.
I've got to clean out his cage, too. Suddenly a light bulb of
questionable wattage appeared over my head. DING! Use the

Hoover to clean out the cage! Save time and fuss! You will go to the park after all, Cinderella!

I shot over to the cage and flung open the tiny door. In went the vacuum hose, which on the old canister vacuums was about the size of a sewer pipe. I started to remove the muck from Barry's cage. It was working splendidly until the phone rang. The ringing distracted me. I turned towards the phone, and then what followed was a sound that I shall never forget. It can only be described like this:

*HHUUUUUMMMMMM***TWEET!!SCCCHHLLOORRRPP!!***HHUUUUUMMMMMM* . . .

My blood ran cold and my life flashed before my eyes, which doesn't take long when you're eight. It was so quick that I was tempted to ask for a repeat. ('. . . and now, another chance to see . . .'). Barry had been well and truly bagged. The poor thing had been minding his own business when he was jet propelled into a bag full of crud! When the blood returned to my brain I opened the vacuum and ripped the bag apart. He was alive! Grey, filthy, and disoriented, but alive! And Mum home at any minute! I've got to clean up Barry before she gets here.

I ran into the bathroom, put Barry in the sink, and rinsed him off with warm water. Some bits that soap and water cannot reach had to be scrubbed, which is why my sister's toothbrush was a bit mucky the next time she used it (sorry, sis). I finished restoring Barry to his usual green and yellow colour, and put him back in the cage. Phew! I thought – that was close!

The problem was that Barry never sang another note. He just sat there with staring glassy eyes and a blank expression on his beak until he escaped out the lounge window six months later when my sister was cleaning out his cage without the vacuum. It was an accident, Simon, and I am truly sorry for my sins. I hope you can find it in your heart to forgive me. I feel much better now that this little mystery has been cleared up. Forgiveness please?

Yours in a flap,

85

Dear Simon,

It all happened in the Lower Sixth. I had a best friend called Alan. We were always finding ways of playing practical jokes on each other. But when it ended in Alan getting me suspended for two weeks, we decided enough was enough. However, I was still out for revenge!

One day, I was round at Alan's and we were sitting in the kitchen when someone said, 'Who's a pretty boy, then?' I looked around the room and saw a parrot in a cage by the back-door window. Alan told me that he was looking after the parrot for the next-door neighbours, a very posh Irish couple who had gone back to Ireland for a few weeks.

Alan was pleased with this Panamanian parrot, as it would repeat everything he said (if he said it enough times).

Then it slowly dawned on me what I would do!

Every day, in my lunch hour, I went to Alan's and climbed over the fence to get round to the back of the house. I found that the top part of the kitchen window was always open and so my revenge began!

I dictated to the parrot some of my worse, most offensive Irish jokes. I did this every day for two weeks. Alan didn't catch on – he heard the parrot say some weird stuff sometimes, but he thought it was just his own family being repeated.

When the Irish couple came back home, and collected the parrot, I left Alan's house in rather a hurry!

The next day in school, Alan had a broken nose. He told me he didn't understand why! He thought he'd done a very good job of looking after the parrot! But the Irish couple didn't!

I have never confessed this, and to this day Alan doesn't know why this Irish couple acted so badly towards him.

By the way – they got rid of the parrot a few days later!

So sorry to the parrot – hope it's got a good home with someone who likes Irish jokes.

Sorry to the couple next door – no offence meant.

And most of all, sorry to Alan, whose nose didn't fix straight, and still has a crook in it – please forgive me!

Anon

Leeds

Dear Simon,

Yes, this is yet another dreadful budgerigar confession.

It happened twelve years ago when I was on my first job for British Telecom. I'd been asked to go and fit an extension lead in an old lady's bungalow. After I'd been there for about half an hour the old lady, who we'll call Mrs F., announced that she was going to the shops and asked me if I'd put the kettle on, saying she'd return in half an hour.

I went into the kitchen, filled the kettle with water and put it on the stove. I then promptly forgot all about it, only going back to look twenty minutes later. As soon as I entered the kitchen I realized that although I'd turned on the gas I'd forgotten to light it, because the whole place stunk of gas. I soon got rid of the smell by opening the windows but to my horror I noticed that the budgie, who was in the cage near the cooker, had ceased to be. It was flat on its back with its claws in the air. Filled with panic, I got hold of the budgie and leant it against the side of the cage, propping it up with its bell which was conveniently hanging from the roof. Satisfied that it looked OK, I went back to my telephone extension.

When Mrs F. returned from the shops and went into the kitchen it was only a matter of time before I heard the shriek. Running in I innocently asked what the problem was. 'It's Barry, the budgie,' she said. 'He died last night and now he's back on his perch!'

Do you think Mrs F. and her deceased budgie will ever forgive me?

Yours sincerely,

Hethersett
Norfolk

Dear Simon,

After listening to the confessions on your show, my conscience finally got the better of me and I've decided to own up to something which happened several years ago.

I was about twelve years old at the time and my father bred rabbits (large quantities, around forty or fifty at a time). He would fatten them up and then sell them to the local market. At the time I had no interest in them, other than to eat one occasionally for Sunday lunch.

Anyway, one weekend my father said to my mother, 'Don't bother getting a joint, dear, we'll have a rabbit.' Off he went down the garden to nab an unsuspecting rabbit for the pot. A few minutes later he returned. 'That's saved some time,' he said. 'One of the little devils had got out of its hutch, so I've hit it on the head and it's hanging up in the shed.'

Several hours passed, and the rabbit was skinned and was stewing nicely in the oven. A knock came on the door. 'Oh, Charlie,' cried the next-door neighbour, 'have you seen our Ronnie's pet rabbit – it's got out and he's ever so upset – we think it went in your garden.' Yes, it was Ronnie's rabbit that was stewing away in our oven. 'We'll have a look for it, Mrs Wills,' said my father, knowing he only had to open the oven door. The following morning my father took one of his own rabbits round to console Ronnie.

I just wanted to say, 'Please forgive me, Ronnie, for knowingly eating your pet rabbit, Bugle – he tasted absolutely delicious. I made a key-ring out of his tail – so if for sentimental reasons you'd like it, just let me know.'

Linda

P.S. I've since turned vegetarian.

BUGLE

Southampton

Dear Simon,

I know you love getting confessions about people's pets. This one is about my mum, she collects rare budgies and mynah birds. Last year her prized possession was a £500 mynah which regularly wandered around the living room for exercise.

One day when Mum was out, I was hoovering and watching TV at the same time but I looked down to see the cleaner sucking up the mynah bird.

I emptied the vacuum bag but the bird was dead and mangled. To be honest I panicked, imagining what Mum would do to me. Firstly I washed off the blood and carpet fluff, but it still looked too bedraggled, so I dried it with a hairdryer and stuffed it in the cage.

When Mum got back, I said casually: 'Your bird doesn't look very well.'

She still thinks the bird dropped dead from a heart attack.

Do you think my mum will forgive me?

All For Love

More plays, more songs, more films, and, yes, more confessions are inspired by affairs of the heart than anything else. Except alcohol. So if you're in love and drunk, stand by for some serious trouble. As 10c.c. said, "AAAAAAH-HHHH, the things we do for love".

Chippenham
Wiltshire

Dear Simon,

My husband is a corporal in the RAF and his name is Del. I feel it is my duty as his wife and co-offender to reveal to the nation and his hangar the secret he has hidden for sixteen years. This pillar of the community, school governor and Star Trek fan should, I feel, unburden himself of his big secret.

It was way back in 1977. He wore flares and a Crimplene jacket. I was, well, perfect... We were both poor, engaged and waiting for him to join the RAF. We'd spend our evenings sharing half a lager in the local pub. We both lived with our families and time alone was scarce, so the shop front of Smith's shoe shop in the town, with its walk-in style cubbyhole window was the ideal place for a snog on a cold winter's night.

This particular night the rubbish was piled up in our little corner of the shop front, ready for the morning collection. It didn't stop us. After a snogging session, we lit up the inevitable fag, adjusted our dress and left.

The next morning, however, the town was buzzing with the news of the big fire. Yes, Smith's had burnt down in the night. Cause unknown! Thankfully, no one was hurt, but Smith's was – well, not much was left...

I feel we shall both benefit by this secret being aired. I know he will at work.

He has other secrets, but this is a family show, I know.

We beg forgiveness.

From,

Debbie

Poole

Dear Simon,

This confession is on behalf of two friends of mine, Phil and Rod. They don't seem to feel in the least bit guilty about it, in fact they seem to find it rather funny, but I will let you be the judge.

The story begins at the local town's rugby club post-defeat celebration. Our two heroes started chatting up two local girls who, for once, chatted back. Now Phil and Rod would not have full dance cards at a Neanderthal Hallowe'en Ball, but the girls appeared to enjoy their company and the evening started to go with a swing. Closing time came and the offer of a cup of coffee back at Rod's place was accepted.

Rod at this time lived in his parents' house, a large and rambling place out in the sticks. What happened in the lounge that night was a little hazy, but after a few cups of coffee, a long and intense debate on philosophical methods, and a certain amount of rather juvenile rummaging around, the girls called a cab and left. Phil and Rod then staggered to bed with self-satisfied smirks on their faces.

The next day the lounge looked as if Motorhead had trashed it. Strewn around the floor were cushions, unwashed cups, cigarette ends, and small pieces of shredded material that looked suspiciously like the remains of a pair of tights. In the middle of the floor was a pair of rather distinctive red shoes that one of the girls must have left in her hurry to get away from the gruesome twosome. Brilliant! A trophy to show the lads at the club!

Phil and Rod went back to the club that lunchtime with their trophy, Rod's sister Julia tagging along as she fancied a drink. At the club behind the bar was held the clubs' collection of trophies. Since they never won anything sporting these consisted of policemen's helmets, traffic cones, and other things that recorded rather sad moments of personal triumph. While Julia was at the bar getting the round in Phil and Rod told the lads of their particular achievement, embellishing it as one does, and then produced the shoes to the general amazement and admiration of everyone there. The shoes were then passed around to the accompaniment of lots of mature comments such as 'Whaheyyy' and 'Cooorrrrr' etc. The crowd then started to get very loud and boisterous and began an ear-splitting rendition of one of their amazingly witty and original songs about things that most of them had neither seen nor experienced. They swept Rod and Phil across to the bar where to thunderous applause the shoes were handed to the barman who placed them on the shelf of honour beside the four wheel nuts removed from the visiting team's Transit. Cries of 'Speech! Speech!' followed, and gradually the noise died down. It was at this point that Rod's sister piped up for all to hear in her rather plummy voice, 'Rod, what are you doing with Mummy's shoes?'

A second of stunned silence was followed by everyone in the room, apart from Rod, Phil and Julia, falling about laughing. Mustering as much dignity as possible Rod quietly took the shoes back from the barman and without a word of explanation walked out.

Yours ashamed for even knowing them,

Keith

Dear Simon Mayo,

I am nineteen years old. I feel I must confess to an incident that took place when I was only sixteen and at my secondary school. At the time I had what I thought were special feelings towards the English master at my school. His name was Mr P. I got it into my head that he liked me a lot by the way that he would smile at me. He was much older than me but I still couldn't help feeling deep stirring at the bottom of my soul whenever he started to talk about grammar.

Bearing this in mind I cannot help feeling guilty for what happened at one of the school's Christmas discos. As usual the disco was boring. The music was old and there were not many lights, and so there were only a few people on the dance floor. I built up a little courage and went up to ask Mr P. whether he would dance with me. I didn't expect him to say yes, but he did. We danced for a bit and he was smiling as usual. After a while, Mr P. had to leave the dance floor because some boys had been found smoking in the changing rooms. I followed him out, and after he had dealt with the smokers he went into the changing rooms, I presume to see everything was intact. I crept in to the changing rooms, and turned the key which he had left in the door. He sprung around at the noise of the key turning, and gave a startled yelp. 'Oh, it's you, Sally,' he said, 'what do you want?'

Well, I thought that I would dive in at the deep end and so I asked him whether he liked me or not. He replied with an 'Eh What?' I could see he was confused, so I repeated the question. When what I was saying had sunk in, instead of answering me in any way he said something along the lines of 'Well, got to go', and made a spring for the door. He reached it and found it was locked, with the air of a criminal, who, standing in front of a firing squad, finds his bindings loose, only to discover someone has just shouted 'Aim . . . Fire'. Agitated is the word I'm looking for. He turned around and as I saw his eyes darting around the room for other escape routes I felt embarrassed and kind of let down. I lost what might be called my marbles for an instant.

Mr P. must have seen something in my eyes, because he was backing off rapidly, and, with the heat of the moment and all that, I gave chase. The confines of my old school changing rooms were small to say the least, and as we approached the eighth or ninth lap and last bench hurdle a key turned in the door and there stood the school janitor. Because the room is small, and Mr P. had got a good lead under starters orders, it looked to this janitor as though Mr P. was chasing me. This janitor was a righteous bod, and wouldn't stand for any of that kind of thing, and so he reported it to the headmaster immediately.

Mr P. got suspended for three weeks without pay because I was so embarrassed I wouldn't speak up.

I confess all now, however, and I would just like to say sorry to Mr P. and say to the headmaster involved that I think three weeks was a bit stiff.

Am I forgiven?

Somewhere in Essex

Dear Father Simon,

My confession goes back seven years.

Being the jealous type and wondering why my husband was eager to get a lift with a certain colleague to work, I decided to investigate further.

After my husband, we'll call him Dick, had fallen asleep, I sneaked down to the cloakroom and rummaged through his work jacket to find his diary. I was feeling very guilty not trusting him but after reading the first page my worst fears were confirmed. It seemed that Dick was having an affair, with the girl, we'll call her Lucy, who lived round the corner. Boy, was I livid! I felt all my emotions were about to burst. But being a shy, quiet type, I decided to seek revenge in my own way.

I often took Percy, my dog, out for late-night walks. Right, I thought, here is my perfect chance. Pottering around the house I found a large tin of white emulsion paint, and my plan was put into action. Later that night I decided to take Percy out for his usual walk. I bid Dick a loving farewell and set off armed with a Tesco carrier with my tin of paint in it, all hidden under my thick winter coat. It was a hot summer evening, but Dick didn't even notice my coat. I headed off towards Lucy's flat to put my plan in motion.

Five minutes later I was walking up the long path to Lucy's flat. Rounding the corner, to my joy, there it stood, Lucy's little brown Ford Fiesta. Being careful to look that no one was around, I told Percy to sit and stay and took the tin of paint from the carrier bag and carefully took off the lid. Being on my guard I took another quick look around and all was clear. I lifted the tin of paint and with great satisfaction poured it all over the windscreen and bonnet of Lucy's brown Fiesta. Feeling satisfied with myself I thought that revenge was sweet. I collected Percy and started the journey home and on the way I threw the empty paint tin over a garden fence.

The next day Dick came home from work full of the story of Lucy's car and the fact that some rotter, those were not his exact words, had vandalized it. To my horror I learnt that the police had been called and helped Lucy remove most of the paint, apart from a few spots here and there. 'Oh dear,' I said, 'have they any idea who did it?' I tried to sound very concerned, but was relieved to hear that they didn't and probably never would find the culprit.

The little car was erased from my mind for the next couple of weeks and Dick seemed to see less of Lucy and on top of all this I passed my driving test first time round, and all seemed rosy.

I was looking for a car myself and later that evening Dick came home very eager for me to close my eyes and come outside to have a look at what he'd bought me. Being the loving wife I did as he asked, but when I opened my eyes I got the biggest shock of my whole life - there in front of me stood Lucy's little brown Fiesta, still with the little white spots intact. I was shocked, no, I can say I was flabbergasted!

Dick explained that it had taken him a couple of months to talk Lucy into parting with her beloved car and that she had let him have it at a real good price because the white spots seemed to spoil the rest of the car. Lucy's boyfriend, whom I must admit I didn't know she had, had given it an M.O.T. and four new tyres.

So, Simon, I am asking forgiveness for having such wicked thoughts about Dick and Lucy and for such a dastardly crime which I think backfired on me anyway and also Lucy, sorry that you spent so much on washing-up liquid to get the paint off my car.

Can I be forgiven?

Yours hopefully,

ANON.

Dear Father Mayo,

I am writing to seek forgiveness for an incident which took place about thirteen years ago, while I was a student at Goldsmiths College, University of London. As I remember, there were four of us involved, whom we shall call Eric and Ernie, Janet (my girlfriend) and John (me). Names have been changed to protect the guilty!

In need of fresh cultural stimulation and cerebral challenges beyond those offered by the bar and the Space Invaders machine, inspiration struck when a colleague returned from a trip to the local joke shop with a paper bag full of little bangers – not fireworks, merely little twists of paper containing something mildly explosive which emitted a sharp but harmless bang when thrown or squeezed between finger and thumb.

To such giant intellects as ours, these seemed a wonderful diversion, and also might, we hoped, take Ernie's mind off snotty Linda, a reasonably attractive brunette, whose chief attributes were a pert behind and a nose carried at 45° as if there were a bad smell permanently underneath it. Poor Ernie was smitten, but was too shy to do more than gaze adoringly at her from afar, and was badly in need of a distraction.

Vast quantities of bangers were duly acquired, but we soon tired of simply throwing them at each other, feeling the need to do something more constructive with them. After much debate, the plot was hatched and the four of us found ourselves outside the women's toilets on the first floor. Janet was sent in as a scout and emerged to report that the coast was clear, whereupon the other three of us slipped surreptitiously in and selected one of the three cubicles as the scene of our crime.

As I'm sure you will have noticed, Simon, most toilet seats have four little rubber studs on the underside, on which the seat rests when it's down. With the seat raised, four bangers were placed strategically on the porcelain and the seat carefully lowered, so that each stud rested on a banger. This accomplished, we retired hastily to a nearby kitchenette and waited.

Well, we didn't have to wait very long. A couple of minutes later, a female figure appeared down the corridor and made its way into the toilets. From behind the kitchenette door it was difficult to be certain of her identity, but there was something very familiar about that pert behind and the nose carried at 45°, and the look of horror on Ernie's face said it all. Yes, it was snotty Linda!

All was not yet lost for Ernie – there was only a one in three chance that she'd choose the booby-trapped cubicle. We waited. A door closed. A bolt latched. There was a slight pause – and a loud bang followed by a hysterical scream . . . Seconds later, snotty Linda emerged and made off down the corridor at about fifty miles an hour, still rearranging her clothing and screaming hysterically. Three of the four of us were hysterical too – we fell about – but poor Ernie just stood there aghast. He had blown up the love of his life . . .

After that, Ernie could never look her in the eye again, even though she was quite unaware of the identity of her tormentors. Although I'm sure we did him a big favour really, it's him I'm seeking forgiveness from, not snotty Linda!

Yours sincerely,

John

(aka someone entirely different)

Somewhere in Lanarkshire

Dear Simon,

In 1981, when I was nineteen, I lived and worked in London, and got myself engaged to Ralph, who was an overseas buyer of sports equipment for a well-known chain of leisure outlets. In addition to being tall, bronzed, with a beautiful body and a black belt in karate — a real macho man — he could also provide me with frequent trips abroad when he had to go buying. So I had many weekends in Paris, the odd week in Spain and Italy, and even three weeks in Sydney, Australia.

Then came the big trip. He was picked to go to America for five months, travelling around, buying gear. I was all set to jack in my job and go with him, but he talked me out of this, pointing out that I would lose my chance of promotion, ruin my career — and, he emphasized, he saw my career as being as important as his — and besides, he would be too busy to spend much time with me. Being a little green, I agreed with him, and stayed behind in London.

Then a mutual friend, who had driven Ralph to the airport, told me that Ralph had taken A.N. Other to the States with him.

I was mildly annoyed, all the more so because I couldn't wreak the kind of revenge I wanted to. His house was locked up for the duration, heavily alarmed, and I didn't have a key, so no going round and calling the weather in New York and leaving the phone off the hook, or leaving the taps running.

Then I recalled that Mr Macho Ralph had one phobia — and I mean phobia — which reduced him to a quivering wreck. I went to the petshop, bought two breeding pairs of mice, dropped them through his letter box, and left them to get on with it. I sneaked round each night after dark to drop food through the door for the wee beasties.

Ralph, in the end, was away for seven months, during which time I got his 'Sorry, I've met someone else' letter.

Finally, the great day came when he came home. The same mutual friend who had driven him to the airport, collected him. Ralph got to his house, de-activated the elaborate alarm system (which wasn't working anyway, because the mice had chewed the wiring), opened the door, and stepped inside, with his arm round his new lady.

When he saw the evidence of the mice, he freaked. He was so terrified he wet himself. His new girlfriend was not impressed. Ralph had to call in Rentokil to get rid of the mice, but even then, he couldn't bear to stay in the house because he knew the mice had been there, and he was forced to put the house on the market. It took ages to sell, as the neighbours – who had never liked Ralph – made sure potential buyers knew all about the rodent infestation. In the end, he had to drop the asking price by £2,500 to get the place sold.

After all these years, I have got to admit that I feel guilty . . . about the fate of the mice, who were after all the innocent victims in all of this, and who met such an untimely end. Do you think I can be forgiven?

Yours, penitently,

Wareham
Dorset

Dear Simon,

I feel I have to write to you to confess something that was to change the course of my life.

On leaving school in 1976 at the tender age of sixteen, I found myself in full-time employment at a large hairdresser's in Poole. At that time the salon was the busiest, trendiest around and therefore employed thirty plus worldly-wise young women whose nightly activities were second to none. On hearing of their conquests in the staff room, I started to think of how I could be noticed and become a contender for some of their attention.

Being a shy, naive boy, how could I accomplish this? I had noticed that the more popular employees sported a number of red blemishes on their necks. These marks of passion, known to us as love bites, would be just what I needed to get noticed as a hot-blooded male. Never having experienced the delights of a woman in any shape or form, how could I achieve the markings of a stud?

I practised on my arm for a number of weeks with some success, but I realized that the problem would be getting the marks onto the neck region (not being a giraffe). Then it came to me. I left work inspired by my inventive thoughts.

When I got home, I headed straight for the garden shed where I cut off an eight-inch length of my father's garden hosepipe. Placing one end in my mouth and the other on my neck, I sucked until I thought my neck would burst. On examining the result, I was so delighted I gave myself three more.

Looking like I'd been kissed by a guppy, I set off for work the next day. From that moment on, my life changed and the talk of the salon was, 'Who was the girl with the perfectly rounded mouth?' From then on I was considered a man, finally noticed by the fairer sex and I never looked back.

I am now the manager of a local salon and therefore seek forgiveness from my old colleagues for deceiving them, from my dad for cutting up his hosepipe, but particularly from the women whom I misled so as to gain my credibility.

Yours hopefully,

S.

Professional Misconduct

Some confessions are motivated by great remorse and some by fear of discovery. The ones in this chapter though are told more glee-fully than most and are motivated I think by a desire to gloat and swagger. Somehow a sin is not a sin if it is committed at work. To be read with chin up and hand on hip.

Somewhere in N.A.T.O.

Dear Father Mayo,

I must seek absolution for the following, which occurred in the summer of 1990. I am a military police dog handler and at the time was serving at several bases in Western Europe. I'd made friends with Maria, who lived near one particular base, and I used to 'pop round most evenings to make sure she was OK'.

Maria had recently bought Rambo, an Alsatian dog who had been abandoned at the local dogs' home. He proved to be badly behaved and Maria had been taking him to obedience classes for weeks without much success. One evening she came home in tears; the instructor had finally lost patience with Rambo and told Maria that unless Rambo's behaviour improved dramatically, the following week would be the last for both of them. They were humiliated in front of all the other dogs and handlers.

Clearly, Simon, some sort of revenge was required and that night, influenced by several lagers, a plan was formulated. The following week I took the dog to the class, where he behaved perfectly, obeying all the instructor's directions, much to his disbelief. However, the instructor wasn't convinced that it was a permanent improvement so I said, 'I've been teaching him to be a guard dog, would you like a demonstration?'

The instructor simply laughed and said, 'That dog could never guard anything.' Simon, that was the cue for action. I wish to confess that the Alsatian with the unusually large teeth that pinned the instructor to the ground with his jaws around the poor man's neck was not Rambo but Max, my highly trained and slightly psychotic guard dog who has been trained to bite hard without breaking the skin.

I'm told the teethmarks stayed for several days on the instructor's neck and he became a nervous wreck, especially near Alsatians. But revenge was sweet. Rambo is just as unruly now but I think justice was done. Can the panel forgive me for illegal use of a lethal weapon? I must remain anonymous for obvious reasons.

Yours in hope,

THE PHANTOM POLICEMAN

ABSENT FRIEND

Westbury Sub Mendip
Somerset

Dear Father Simon,

This is a confession dating back to when Harold Wilson was the Prime Minister.

I have the ability to change my voice and do reasonably acceptable impersonations. I do a remarkable impersonation of Harold Wilson and that will form the central storyline of this confession.

At the time I was employed by a local authority in South Yorkshire and shared an office with an equally deranged lawyer. We were always looking for lively and harmless pranks and one wet Thursday afternoon we chose the subject of football for our next prank.

My colleague therefore telephoned the secretary of Huddersfield Town Football Club, introduced himself as the Prime Minister's private secretary and said the Prime Minister would like a short word.

I said good morning to the secretary, in my excellent Harold Wilson voice. The secretary said 'Good morning, sir, how can I help you?'

I said, I shall be visiting the constituency on Saturday and as I would have two or three hours spare before my evening appointment thought it would make a nice relaxing change to watch a game of football. I asked if seats could be reserved in the Directors' Box and if tickets could be sent to 10 Downing Street together with car parking passes.

The secretary assured me that no tickets would be necessary but that car parking permits would be sent so that my chauffeur could drive straight into the Directors' car parking area without question and someone would be briefed to greet us on arrival.

I said thank you very much and terminated the call.

Sitting down to watch the local TV sports programme on the following Saturday, I was taken completely by surprise when the sports commentator of that time - Keith Macklin - introduced the day's big game from Huddersfield Town's ground.

He gave all the usual introductions and then said - 'We are expecting the Prime Minister here today' - at which point the camera lens swung round to the Directors' Box to reveal two empty seats flanked by very well turned out directors and gentry, all obviously looking forward to meeting Harold Wilson. What a disappointment they were in for, I thought.

Needless to say Harold Wilson never turned up, everybody was disappointed but I have to say my colleague and I awarded ourselves a full 20 points for the prank because clearly the secretary must have telephoned Yorkshire Television after our call and of course YTV must have gone to some reasonable amount of trouble and expense to arrange short-notice coverage of that game, purely to get old Harold in the picture.

My confession ends there and whereas I do not really seek overwhelming forgiveness hope that same will be forthcoming. After all these years I thought it would be good to share the experience with your listeners, apologize to Keith Macklin, Yorkshire Television and most of all to the then secretary of Huddersfield Town Football Club.

Regards,

Philip

Dear Simon,

Back in the early 1970s I started a job as a pollution control officer looking after a large well-known river in central Scotland (which rhymes with Slide). Jobs were hard to come by and the River Purification Board set very high standards for their employees – in fact they made it abundantly clear to me that if I didn't perform miracles during my six months probationary period, I'd be out on my ear. I was desperate to impress so the word 'failure' was eradicated from my dictionary.

One of my first jobs was to investigate the source of minor oil contamination of the pristine upper reaches of this magnificent river. I quickly traced it to a drainage pipe in the river bank but couldn't easily establish which of three nearby oil-using premises was discharging the oil into this pipe. I dared not return to my headquarters without being able to report that I had traced and stopped the oil – especially as the local radio station and newspapers were pressuring my boss for a statement about the incident. I knew that one sure-fire way of testing if a premises was connected to a particular pipe, was to put a special harmless dye into a drain at the premises and see if the colour turned up in the pipe at the river – simple as that!

I had a gallon of concentrated fluorescent red dye in my van for just this purpose, so I set to work at once. I unscrewed the stopper and thought, 'Hmmmm, I've never used this stuff before . . . I wonder how much I should use?' To play safe, I just poured in half a cupful but when, after waiting an hour, the colour hadn't appeared at the river, I decided to slosh the whole gallon in.

Ten minutes later an incredible garish red colour spouted forth into the river from the drain, which turned the entire width of the river pale pink for about fifteen minutes before fading away to nothing. What a shock I had, but after regaining my composure, I felt quietly pleased with myself and marched confidently into the polluter's premises and gave them a right royal rollicking and got them to stop the cause of the oil discharge immediately.

I returned to the river bank in the certain knowledge that the oily discharge should have stopped and the river should have been perfect again.

Well, the oil had stopped . . . but it wasn't perfect – it was blinding red in colour. The sunlight reflecting off it lit the whole valley up a rosy red – miles and miles of a gigantic fluorescent scarlet ribbon winding its way through one of the most beautiful landscapes in Britain. I realized what I had done – the first wee drop of dye caused the river to turn pink and an hour behind it came a whole gallon – it was just like the film The Ten Commandments when Moses dipped his staff into the sea.

As I mentioned earlier, the dye was harmless, but that was no consolation to thousands of pink fish, and owners of pink rowing boats, and several farmers who owned pink and black sheepdogs and cattle with pink legs and heads.

Best wishes,

Chris

Glasgow

Dear Father Simon,

In 1969, as a poor student, I went to work as a waiter in a four-star hotel in Wester Ross in northwest Scotland — at least it WAS a four-star hotel — to earn some bread to help me survive the impecunious months as a student. Booze costs money!

We worked astonishingly long hours in the dining room, some days from 7.30 am to 11.00 pm — no kidding — with only a few short breaks! There was always a huge sigh of relief at around 10.00 pm as the last guests left as we could then prepare the dining room for breakfast before we retired to the bar for a few well-earned pints.

Imagine our dismay when one evening at around 10.15 pm a group of about a dozen well-oiled but rich and patronizing punters slimed through the door and browbeat our head waiter to allow them to have dinner outwith the normal time!

They then proceeded to order a full à la carte meal which was obviously going to take all night to prepare, serve and clean up after — far less organize things for breakfast! We were not impressed. The head waiter was not impressed — but he was hoping for a big tip! The chef was not impressed! Still we went ahead. I now need to set the scene for those who have never had a look in the kitchen of a large hotel! Most kitchens have large steel baths which are used to store tureens of soups and sauces, etc. to keep them hot but not cooking in the nearly boiling water. Because the hotel was four-star we were all well trained in silver service and one of the problems in a busy dining room was to be able to keep one's silver fork and spoon twinkly clean for serving the next diner — not easy if mashed tatties had just been dispensed! It became a ritual for staff waiting for their table's food to be produced from the kitchen to rinse their implements in the hot water and dry them on a napkin ready to serve the next dish. Needless to say, although the bath was cleaned out every two weeks or so it was a fairly foul-looking brew.

Needless to say, one of the guests ordered consommé — a kind of clearish meat-based soup very popular with the so-called gourmet set! Horrors! None left except a dribble at the bottom of the tureen! Eddie, a Swiss chef of incredible temper but great inventiveness, poured out the dribble onto a soup plate, but not enough! With a flourish he swept a ladleful of dishwater from the bath into the tureen, but said, 'Not brown enough!' A spoonful of chocolate sauce was added and mixed and melded with the dribble of consommé. 'Voila!' quoth Eddie. It was served, eaten and cleared up! We laughed for hours! I'm not really looking for absolution as they left a miniscule tip so they – or at least one of them – got what they deserved!

Mac.

Bristol

Dear Father Simon,

I would like to free myself of a burden that I have carried with me since 1987.

It was when I had the exquisite pleasure of working on a fresh fish counter in a large supermarket, which shall remain nameless as I wouldn't want to offend Gateway.

The job entailed a very early start, at 7 am, when we (me and my two chums) would completely fill the eighteen foot counter with crushed ice, which was mass-produced by a very temperamental ice-maker in the prep. room, then lay out, in a very beautiful display, all sorts of fish, some whole, some filleted and some sliced. The displays were our pride and joy, scenes of fish eating smaller ones, salmon swirling in spirals and smoked fish in wide fan shapes, all dotted with bunches of parsley and slices of lemon.

However, the centre of the service counter was raised higher than the rest and at an angle of 30° and had to have whole fresh rainbow trout in vertical rows covering the entire centrepiece. Now, this looked fine albeit lacking in imagination, so we decided to liven it up a bit – literally!!

One day, when business was slower than usual and boredom was setting in, I came up with the perfect way to brighten our day.

I managed to obtain a very long piece of wire from another department and carefully hooking the end into a trout's eye I ran the wire under the head, under the ice, over the top of the counter and along the back to the end, where I stood looking bored and uninterested (as is required of most super-market staff!!).

The wire was completely out of sight of the customers and so when a young family approached, the wicked but hilarious plan went into action.

As often happens in supermarkets, the adults were chatting, oblivious to their little darlings' exploits, and so the sight of whole, slimy, wet fish, eyes and all, was irresistible to one little boy who came over to have a closer look. Just as his hot little hand came within a trout's nose's distance of the fish, I jerked the wire and the head twitched perfectly in mock death throes.

I have several points on which I would like to be forgiven:

1. For putting the parents in the embarrassing position of having to calm down a near-hysterical child in the middle of a supermarket.
2. From the child who received a rather hefty whack for telling lies about the trout, who, incidentally, had suddenly and mysteriously become inert

once again.

3. And finally from the trout, whose life ended only to be a party to my evil fishy frolics.

Lots of love and fishy fingers,

Billinghurst
Sussex

Dear Father Simon,

I feel that the time has come for me to publicly confess to a great sin that I committed some two years ago. I do not expect forgiveness from you, as I cannot even begin to forgive myself.

At the time of my dreadful deed, I was working for a company in Barry, South Wales, as a sales engineer, and spent most of my time travelling the UK selling labelling machinery. Approximately once a week, I had to visit the office to catch up on paperwork, discuss various projects with the boss, etc. This journey from Sussex took about three hours each way, and became more and more tedious.

On this particular occasion, I had left home at 6 am and spent until 4.30 in the office. Finishing my list of things to do for the day, my attention turned to getting home as quickly as possible to my two children (my dear wife having left me and the kids some time before for my best friend made this even more important).

I jumped into my car, and drove as quickly as possible out of the industrial area of Barry to join the main Barry-Cardiff road. Locals will know that this road consists of short stretches and seven roundabouts.

As I approached the Cardiff road at the second roundabout, I had to turn right, thus giving me the right of way over traffic approaching from the left (i.e. from Barry town). However, as I hit the roundabout, a funeral procession was approaching. Even though it was 'my' road, my natural instinct was to stop and allow the hearse to go first.

I braked, but then remembered the other five roundabouts. I would be stuck behind the procession for ages. It was too bad to think about.

I instantly changed my mind, and accelerated round the roundabout in front of the hearse – causing the driver to brake. The chief mourners' car did not brake, and drove straight into the back of the hearse!

What could I do? Keep going, of course! My last view in the

mirror was of the hearse driving off again, the mourners' car trying to follow, with its front bumper dragging along the ground.

Please Simon, forgive me. I still wake at night with this terrible deed weighing heavily on my conscience. And even more important, please don't read out my name, for obvious reasons.

Richard

Dear Father Simon,

Please can you help me purge my soul and conscience of the memory of two events that happened on the same day in 1972 when I was a police officer in a large constabulary in the North of England?

The first event probably demonstrates what planks the police employed at that time, but the second . . . well, words fail me . . .

One morning I was late for work and on arriving at 6.30 am instead of 6.00am I was rewarded with the job of giving the prisoners their breakfasts.

We had to collect the breakfasts from the fire station across the road and it always consisted of a large jug of steaming tea and some hot bacon sand-wiches. Down I merrily went into the cell block with the tea, etc. and went into a cell which was set aside for sorting out the prisoners' meals – pouring out the tea into cups and putting the sandwiches on plates. As I entered the cell I kicked the cell door behind me (hoping just to close it slightly) and heard it gently shut and of course the lock engage. My heart sank. Not to worry, I thought, I've got a very large bunch of keys with me for all the cell doors.

I then realized that cell doors don't in fact have a keyhole on the inside (I was only young at the time) and so for the next twenty minutes wondered what to do. In desperation I decided to press the alarm button and had to be rescued by a fellow officer whom I swore to silence.

As for the prisoners' breakfasts – well, by this time the tea was stone cold and the bacon sandwiches horribly congealed, so I would like to confess to the prisoners that it was in fact my fault and that I was being slightly economical with the truth when I told them loudly, 'Sorry, lads, but those prats at the fire station couldn't organize a . . . etc.' But worse was to follow!

Later the same morning I spotted on the police station notice board details of a parade by Scouts and Guides that day and realized that I was supposed to be on point-duty at a particularly busy road junction to stop the traffic for the parade about ten minutes later. I left the station rapidly and arrived at this junction just in time to confirm on my radio that I was in position.

Shortly I heard the sound of bugles and kazoos approaching and could see about 100 Scouts and Guides marching up the road towards me. At this point I suddenly realized that I had read the notice in the Police Station so quickly that I didn't have a clue which way the march was supposed to go at my junction. Common sense would have told you that they would probably be heading for the town centre, but at that moment any common sense I had went straight out of the window.

What did I do? Well, naturally I stopped all the traffic and directed the parade straight up the dual carriageway towards the M62 motorway! Seeing the youngsters march off into the distance I did what anyone would have done under the circumstances. I legged it, Father Simon, reappearing at the police station some hours later with a severe case of 'Sorry, Sergeant, but these radio batteries are useless, they don't last ten minutes now'.

Now maybe the prisoners' breakfasts fiasco wasn't the end of the world. But I have this recurring image of a group of about 100 ten-to-fourteen-year-olds – our future generation – possibly being mowed down by a juggernaut and all my fault. Only you can forgive this transgression. Help me, Father, for I have sinned.

Yours repentantly,

An ex-Police Officer

Birmingham

Dear Simon,

I am aware that you are keen to obtain medical confessions so here goes.

My story begins in my junior house officer days (first hospital job, 96 hours per week, no sleep, etc., etc.)

A patient (who shall be known as Mr A) was admitted to the ward where I was working. He was unconscious at this time and was put into a bed next to another man who I shall call Mr B. Mr B was a very old and frail man. The nurses made great efforts to persuade him to eat, but with no success. One day a very dedicated and caring student nurse was given the job of persuading him to eat his dinner. In a blinding flash of inspiration she realized that Mr B's lack of appetite was due to the fact that he was not wearing his false teeth. Without hesitation she picked up the teeth from the bedside table and placed them in Mr B's mouth.

Unfortunately this did not improve matters and later that night Mr B passed away. I was called upon to confirm that he was dead, which I did, and the porters took him to the morgue where he would stay until funeral arrangements could be made.

The same night, but a little later, Mr A (who, you will remember, was unconscious on admission) woke up. A miraculous recovery. However, he was not well pleased. 'Where are my f***ing teeth?' he cried.

I was called out of bed to see this aggressive patient and managed to calm him down saying that his teeth would be somewhere on the ward and that we would find them. The nursing sister, several junior nurses and myself frantically searched the ward for the missing teeth. Laundry baskets were emptied, drawers were overturned and patients' lockers were searched. All to no avail.

Eventually the awful truth dawned on me. The bedside table was between Mr A's and Mr B's bed and, yes you guessed it, in the nurse's enthusiasm she had given Mr B the teeth belonging to Mr A. The teeth were not on the ward but in the morgue!

Hospital morgues are not pleasant places to wander around in the middle of the night, but I couldn't face the wrath of Mr A when I told him what had happened to his teeth. So I crept into the morgue, found Mr B's body and removed the teeth from his mouth. With my heart still pounding I rushed back to the ward with my booty. I washed the teeth and took them to Mr A. 'Look,' I said 'we've found them! I told you we would. They were in the laundry basket all along,' I lied. 'I guess the cleaners must have thrown them in there by mistake.'

I often think of the poor unfortunate man who, to this day, is wearing teeth that were rescued from Mr B. So Simon, I beg forgiveness, not from Mr A who was a fat, rich and foul-mouthed man and deserved everything he got, but from Mr B and his family for disturbing him, and from the cleaner whom I had blamed for the mishap.

Yours sincerely,

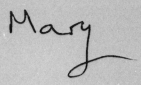

Mary

Markfield

Dear Simon,

This is a confession of a friend of mine from when we used to work together in a hotel. Every Saturday throughout the summer we had a contract with a coach company which brought pensioners from the North-east to the south coast for a summer holiday. As the hotel was situated in the Midlands, just two minutes from the M1, we were the ideal place to stop for lunch.

The coach company were pleased with the arrangements for we provided an excellent three-course meal with coffee at a reasonable price, and did not seem to mind if the coach was delayed en route. The staff however did not feel the same way. The meal was more like musical chairs than a respectable lunch. After twenty minutes of deciding who was to sit where, over half of them remembered they wanted to go to the loo, and the others had left their teeth on the coach. Questions like 'Would you like any wine?' were often met with 'It's a quarter past two, lovey'. I must admit we did play on this slightly, like when asked by a respectable gent if he could have a gin and tonic for his wife, we would tell him, 'Sorry, we don't do swaps'.

On this particular day, after the normal shuffle round, and the 'hold on, I want to sit next to Elsie' routine, we started to serve the soup. Cream of tomato, mmm lovely. As you probably know, waiters have a way of holding three soup bowls, two in one hand and one in the other. My friend leant round one lady to serve her soup, but when straightening up he noticed, to his surprise, the top bowl of the other two was empty. The red trace left in the bowl showed it had tipped out while he was serving the first. He looked down and saw it had poured, quite neatly, into an open handbag. Without hesitation he did what all well-trained waiters do – he said nothing and shut the bag with his foot.

The rest of the meal went without a hitch, and we all lined up to watch the old biddies climb back aboard their coach, resisting the temptation to tap our soup smuggler on the shoulder, and arrest her for 'shoplifting'.

All this happened over fifteen years ago. Do you think the soup smuggler forgave us? Would you?

Altrincham
Cheshire

Dear Father Simon,

I plead for forgiveness from you for what can only be described as a crime against half of Manchester's residents on a cold winter's evening in December 1988. There is no need to disguise my name as the event was thoroughly published in all the news-papers and television bulletins on the fateful evening of Friday 23rd December. At this time in my life I was a traffic policeman with the Greater Manchester Police Motorway Unit and I had been serving in my new post for just a couple of weeks. It was my first week in my new job and was on my own as my regular partner PC John Fitzpatrick was on holiday.

At about 3 pm I was called up to escort a slow-moving wide load containing Boeing 747 aircraft wings from our boundary with the Cheshire Police Force to the far side of Manchester. This type of duty normally fell to the motor cycle unit but they happened to be on Royal Protection duties that day; so the job fell to me.

I eagerly went to meet the load from our counterparts in the Cheshire Police Force who had escorted it from the south of the country and handed responsibility over to me. This was my first day alone on the motorway section so I wished to create a good impression with my superiors. There I was, so proud in my brand spanking new Ford Capri patrol car, taking command of this valuable cargo.

I had not been told of any special route to take by our oper-ations room, so I proceeded along the most direct route from the pick-up point in Altrincham towards Manchester City Centre. This route took me up a slip road onto what is locally known as the Mancunian Way. I raced up the slip road in front of the load in order to halt the traffic on the main flyover to give the load a free run. I activated by blue lights and sirens and the traffic duly came to a halt whilst I waited for the load to appear. I heard an almighty screech of brakes and a horrible crashing and scraping noise that I shall never forget as long as I live.

I suddenly remembered. The slip road I was leading this huge monstrosity up was sixteen feet wide. The load was – nineteen feet wide! The whole vehicle became stuck like a cork in a bottle between the Armco barriers and my immediate thoughts were of doing a runner away from the scene, pretending it had never happened and leaving the poor old driver to sort himself out.

I had to face reality quickly though and summon help. I told the control room what had happened but omitted to tell them that I had led the helpless driver up the unauthorized route for wide loads and instead informed them that he had disobeyed my express instructions NOT to take this route over the Mancunian Way. My senior officers did not wear this and upon their arrival at the scene told me what they thought of my first attempt at escorting wide loads.

The council engineers' department had to be turned out with huge bolt-cutters and specialized welding equipment to remove the barriers. Three specialist crane operators had to be mobilized to lift the immense vehicle and its load off the slip road together with three fire appliances who were put on standby at the scene in case of a fire caused by sparks from the welders. I had interrupted everybody's office Christmas party. They were not pleased. Worse still, all the commuters trying to leave Manchester City Centre after their pre-Christmas lunches were delayed by up to three hours due to my incompetence. All in all I was not a popular young man.

Worse was to come as huge crowds gathered sneering at my misfortune.

The final nightmare arrived in the form of two television crews together with a melee of reporters and photographers from national and local newspapers. This, I thought, was the end of a short career in the traffic unit. Then I remembered that one of the chaps on duty that day was a bit of a wally and I'd had run-ins with him before. His name was Dave and I owed him one from many years previously.

It was at this point that my game plan came into being. I approached a scruffy-looking reporter and said that off the record this type of incident was due to inexperienced young traffic officers not being trained properly. 'Who was responsible for getting this load stuck? Was it you?' he asked. 'No,' I replied. 'Then who was it?' he insisted. 'PC Johnson,' I replied. 'But he's not here at the moment,' I continued.

'It's a chap called Johnson,' I heard him call to the remainder of the assembled hacks. They all took their photographs and compiled their news bulletins and left.

What had I done, I thought to myself. Not only have I interrupted so many people's office Christmas parties and brought the whole of the city centre of Manchester to a standstill but I have lied to the press and got one of my colleagues into trouble.

Four hours later the load was eventually released from the confines of the barriers, having taken

30 council workmen
15 Firefighters
10 Additional police officers and
6 crane operatives

to release it. Needless to say I was not allowed to continue escorting the load to its final destination. The final bill for my little escapade was just in excess of £20,000 and it took me over a week to complete a whole set of written reports into the cause of the incident.

My conscience has however eventually got to me, Father Simon, and I seek forgiveness from the following:

All the people who had to turn out from their office parties in order to release the load, including the workmen, crane operatives and firefighters.
The driver of the lorry who I squarely blamed for having taken a route that I expressly forbade him from taking, this of course being a whopping lie.
But mostly I ask forgiveness from PC Johnson who was not able to defend himself from the snipes of incompetence aimed at him from the various sections of the press.

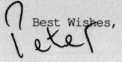

Best Wishes,

Peter

125

Gwent

Dear Simon,

When I was aged seventeen I worked for a small but up-and-coming advertising agency. Times were hard and business was very slow. Things were
looking very bleak when suddenly my company was asked to devise a large
advertising campaign for a multinational company.

This was the break our company needed and we slaved for three months to
produce artwork and ideas for the final presentation. The clients would visit
regularly to see how the work was progressing and my boss was told that
out of all the agencies competing for the vast account we had the most
imaginative ideas and the account could only go to us.

As the deadline for the presentation to the clients grew nearer my boss,
who was a constant chain smoker, became more and more worked up. On
the morning of the presentation I decided to play a joke on him just to take
his mind off what was a very important day. I obtained a box of exploding
tips you put into cigarettes – the sort that go bang and blacken the face of
the smoker – just for a laugh I might add.

I waited for my boss to go out of the room and while he was gone I just
had time to take out one cigarette from his packet left on the desk. I
crammed this cigarette with four exploding tips, not just one as recom-
mended. I thought this would be more fun. I replaced the packet on the
desk and waited to see what would happen.

My boss returned, picked up the packet and went about his business. I chuckled to myself all morning as he smoked another and yet another cigarette, but nothing happened. With all the preparation taking place for the final presentation to our main client at 2.00 pm I forgot all about it.

The presentation went very well and the clients loved the new advertising campaign. As they laughed and joked about the special relationship they wanted with our agency my boss produced a packet of cigarettes from his pocket. He offered one to the company's Managing Director. I really wanted to stop my boss from lighting it for him, but I didn't want to look stupid. As he took the lighter away there was a massive bang. Bits of tobacco flew across the room. The client sat stunned with the tip of the cigarette hanging from his mouth. His face was black with soot and his expensive suit turned from cream to grey.

My boss sat there too, with sheer horror on his face and the look of a man who was about to lose everything. I can't repeat the conversation they had after that, but it started with 'You silly bmmmmr'. The clients stormed out of the room and all of the hard work we had done went down the drain.

It was lucky my boss blamed his twelve-year-old son for the unfortunate incident. It was very unlucky for his son who got a good hiding, couldn't go out for a month and had his school trip to Italy cancelled.

If it's any consolation, I was made redundant a month later due to lack of work. Please forgive me. I have never played a practical joke since and am now a hard-working hotel manager.

Yours faithfully,

127

Stranraer

Dear Simon,

I feel I am now able to reveal to you something I did nigh on twenty-three years ago.

I was fifteen at the time and, having just left school and waiting to go to catering college, I took a seasonal job at a large hotel in Cornwall. If I said the town it would be obvious, as it was the only large hotel there. Suffice to say it begins with F, ends with Y and has O W E in between.

Anyway, at that time tie-dye T-shirts were all the rage, especially the DIY variety. Being 'hip', as I then was, I decided to buy a plain white T-shirt and some dye and have a go myself. The hotel kitchen was always deserted between 2.30 and 5 pm, so I decided this was the best time, as I needed a large pan for the operation. Hauling a huge one from the shelf, I filled it with cold water, salt, the dye and the suitably tied T-shirt, and proceeded to stir the dark blue mixture. Rinsing out the pan, I went back to my room with the dyed shirt in hand, thinking how brilliant it would be when dry and what a 'cool dude' I would look in it.

The chefs at the hotel started earlier in the evening than the KPs, and it was not until about 6 pm that I went to the kitchen to begin work. Three chefs were standing at the stove, all peering into this pan, scratching their heads (not into the pan!) and saying things like, 'What the . . . happened here?' and 'I've never seen anything like this before!'

As I passed them I peered into the vessel and nearly fainted. The pan was full to the top with bright blue potatoes!

Dinner was only an hour away and the head chef screamed at me to get some more potatoes prepared quickly. (Those weren't his exact words.) 'Did anyone see me this afternoon?' I thought, as I peeled the potatoes. I was certain I'd washed the pan out properly, but obviously the dye had gone into the pores of the metal.

Suffice to say, I never wore my tie-dye T-shirt, which I kept hidden in my room. Having now risen to head chef myself, I often think back to that time, but until now have never (unlike the pan) 'come clean' about the 'mystery of the blue potatoes'.

I ask for forgiveness, Simon, for this colourful period of my life and apologize to the chef concerned, who to this day must still wonder about the day the spuds 'dyed'.

Yours apologetically,

TOM

Manchester

Dear Simon,

This is a true confession about an incident that happened in 1980. Only now have I decided to come clean and ask forgiveness for this ghastly deed.

In 1980 I joined the Royal Navy and after basic training I was sent to Rosyth, Scotland, for operational training on board a mine sweeper.

There was a chef on board who used to get rather jealous when after lunch everyone would get their towels and sunbathe on the upper deck for the rest of the lunch break while he was left to wash up. Every now and then he would play a little trick on everyone. He would switch on the electric cooker ring and the extractor fan to the upper deck and would sprinkle a teaspoon of pepper onto the hot ring. This would produce a great cloud of brown smoke that had the same effect as tear gas. He would then run up to the upper deck and have a good laugh as sailors started scattering every which way, crying, scratching, sneezing and cursing.

After this, I was given a week's leave and told to report to a frigate that was in dry dock in Portsmouth for a refit. After a wonderful leave telling all my friends what new and wonderful lands I had discovered whilst away at sea (!), the time came for me to head south, but I overslept and missed my 6 am connection to Portsmouth and ended up twenty minutes late for duty. When this happens in the Royal Navy you are sent to see the Captain. He gave me three days' extra duties and told me not to be late again. So on my first day on a real warship I spent my dinner hour helping the chef, instead of exploring my new surroundings. After everyone had finished lunch, the chef left me to wash up whilst he went onto the upper deck with everyone else to sunbathe. Yes, you've guessed it, my plot was hatched

When the last pot was clean, I found a tin of pepper and switched on the extractor fan and cooker. I punctured the tin at the bottom and a steady trickle of pepper began to flow onto the ring, producing a plume of thick brown smoke that was being sucked up. Wonderful!

I locked the galley door and went to the upper deck to witness my handiwork. But everything was normal: sailors sunbathing, reading and generally relaxing. Unbeknown to me, with the ship being in dry dock, the dockies had removed half the ventilation system for repair, so instead of the smoke going to the upper deck, it had been re-routed to various parts of the ship, i.e. the engine room, bridge, wardroom and stores!

Before I could get back to the galley to switch everything off, the fire alarm rang and pandemonium broke out. After thirty minutes the fire fighting party reported that they had not located the cause of the fire, but the whole ship was filled with smoke, so the Hampshire fire brigade was called in. After a further thirty minutes they finally found the cause of the smoke after breaking down the galley door.

Dear Simon, I do not seek forgiveness for the pain I caused the chef – who got thirty days' extra duties – but I would like to seek forgiveness for the injury I did the captain, who to this day is still known as Captain Dry Dock, as he is the only skipper to abandon ship whilst in dry dock.

Anon

A Temptation Too Far

In the Good Book, we're told that God never lets us be tempted more than we can stand. The evidence of this chapter suggests, a) that this is not true, or b) that some of you are quite happy giving in to it!

Warrington

Dear Father Simon,

It was in the winter of 1985, Father, in the city centre of Liverpool, that I was assigned the very responsible role of 'Tutor Constable' to the new recruit on our section. Due to the need to rely upon each other in a variety of circumstances we developed a very close working bond and, as part of his professional development, I encouraged my colleague to confide in me whenever he felt the need.

Thanks to the plethora of rather traumatic incidents to which he was exposed my colleague took me up on the invitation and regularly poured out his heart to me. I can honestly say, Father, that I fulfilled my role with dedication. However, my young recruit went one disclosure too far. He conveyed to me a very commonly held fear – it was the mind-numbing fear he had of dead bodies and his subsequent dread at the thought of dealing with one in the course of his duties.

Well, Father Simon, such an opportunity was too good to miss and as I possessed a sense of humour common to most police officers, i.e. warped and depraved, I shared this information with the rest of the section and we hatched a cunning plan.

The following week was to be the first that our young colleague, whom I will now refer to as Constable X, was to experience patrolling alone, a threshold in any officer's career and one that did not escape our attention.

Situated in a murky, dimly lit Victorian backstreet was the City Mortuary and it was to this ghoulish location that all of the bodies of people unfortunate enough to pass away during the night were taken and laid out. It was no coincidence that Constable X was posted to the beat that covered the said Mortuary and thus he assumed responsibility for the premises.

It was shortly after 5 am when the radio of Constable X crackled into life, breaking the silence of a cold, wintry night. From the radio room came the instruction to attend at the Mortuary and collect the wedding ring from the hand of Body No. 77 which had been laid out earlier that night by an officer from a neighbouring division who had forgotten to remove the ring when itemizing the deceased person's property.

135

It was a pale and drawn Constable X who walked into the station foyer a short time later to collect the key to the mortuary. As the station keeper passed him the key, lovingly adorned with a small wooden coffin as a key fob, he muttered some reassuring words about ignoring the reputation of the Mortuary as being the haunt of some notorious Liverpool ghosts. Constable X was not convinced and, putting on a brave face, ventured out into the cold night to discharge his unpleasant duty.

A biting wind was howling as Constable X approached the archway at the entrance to the mortuary, poorly lit by a solitary gas light. Nervously he placed the key in the lock and opened the door which, like that of all good mortuaries, was in grave need of a spot of oil. The design of the building was such that you had to walk the length of the main room in order to turn on the lights which, at 5 am and all alone, is something of a trial to those of a nervous disposition.

Constable X switched on his torch and started to walk along the tiled floor. The air was filled with the smell of formaldehyde and several of the bodies were situated on trolleys in front of the refrigerators. Having reached the light switch he turned them on, took a deep breath and turned around. Initially he stood rooted to the spot before gathering himself and moving towards the nearest body that was lying on a trolley, covered by a white sheet.

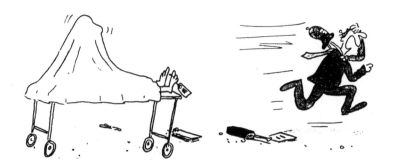

Tentatively he checked the number on the small tag attached to the big toe of the body, protruding from beneath the sheet. Slowly he moved along the bodies until he reached BODY 77. The left hand of the body could just be seen, adorned with the wedding ring that he sought. Even on such a cold night beads of sweat could be detected on the forehead of Constable X and his skin was pale and clammy. It was some time before he had composed himself enough to reach out for the cold, motionless hand. However, as he grasped hold of the said hand he let out a piercing scream and threw himself backwards onto the floor as the body suddenly sat up rigidly and exclaimed, 'CAN I HELP YOU?' Constable X immediately assumed a state of absolute panic, screaming at the top of his voice and scampering backwards on the floor like a double-jointed crab.

Eventually he got back to his feet and sprinted towards the exit of the mortuary. However, his legs soon began to buckle again as, first to his right and then to his left, body after body began to sit up accompanied by much groaning. It was eventually on all fours that he disappeared into the night pursued only by the sound of raucous laughter.

Of course, the 'bodies' in question were in fact the warped work colleagues of Constable X, of whom I was one.

Constable X, traumatized beyond belief, sadly resigned the next day despite our reassurances that he had merely been subjected to an initiation ceremony.

Yours sinfully,

Ray

West Midlands

Dear Simon,

I am asking forgiveness for something that happened in 1989 whilst I was in California. I had joined a Metaphysical church which was full of 'warm, friendly, genuine people' (aren't all Californians warm, friendly, genuine people??). I soon became 'one of the family', and was invited to attend the Rev. Ethel's healing and spiritual development circle. There I sat praying, meditating and talking with those 'warm, friendly, genuine people'. Then came the end of the session, which was dedicated to sending out healing prayers to friends and family. Rev. Ethel spoke the names of two unwell people Jill and Ken. Then to my utter surprise everyone began to sing 'Jill and Ken, Jill and Ken, Jill and Ken.' Little did they know they were singing those names to a well-known 'Watch with Mother' tune.

Finally, it was my turn. The Rev. Ethel solemnly asked me, 'Peter . . . do you have anyone you would like to send out healing prayers to?' I couldn't resist it . . . with tears in my eyes, I uttered the names . . . 'Bill and Ben.'

I would like these 'warm, friendly, genuine people' to forgive me for making them sing Bill and Ben, Bill and Ben, Bill and Ben. Of course I couldn't join in as I was in too much pain from trying to stop myself laughing and adding the words, 'Flowerpot Men' at the end of their little ditty. Am I forgiven?

Yours,

Peter

Melton Mowbray
Leics

Dear Simon,

As my confession involves arson and 'mild' grevious bodily harm (if there are in fact varying degrees of GBH), criminal offences to the best of my knowledge, I would be grateful if you would preserve my anonymity for fear of lawsuits or personal retribution from the parties involved.

It goes back some twelve years to when I was a student at West Bridgford College of Further Education near Nottingham.

Once a fortnight I used to visit a friend in the most rural of backwaters in a village called Harby. My journey there involved catching a bus from Nottingham, dropping people off at numerous small villages en route and terminating at my destination, Harby being the terminus. By this time I was always the last passenger on the bus as hardly anyone even lives in Harby, and there is very little to go there for unless there is a whist drive on at the village hall. At that time (and probably to this day) the drivers for this particular bus company had to live with the misfortune of a uniform consisting of a beige shirt complete with epaulettes and cowpat-brown NYLON trousers and jacket. In short a complete fashion disaster. If this were not bad enough, the trend amongst the drivers, who had an awful tendency to really fancy themselves, was to wear balding greasy hair about eight inches long on one side and then swept over the bald patch. And big Elvis-style sideburns. And copious quantities of Brylcreem.

The absolute worst of these aforementioned sex gods was unfortunately the driver who drove my route on that particular day of the week. He really fancied himself and worse still, he seemed to fancy me and even yet worse, he thought that I fancied HIM. So much so that on my fortnightly journeys he would stop the bus, leaving the engine ticking over, and come and sit and have a little innuendo-filled chat with me. As the weeks passed, his little chat-ups began to include putting his hand on my shoulder and touching my hair – you know the sort of thing. I as an innocent sixteen-year-old felt that he as a repulsive and sad middle-aged man sporting a wedding ring should be very much discouraged from this sort of behaviour and I communicated this verbally to him on numerous occasions. I took to sitting on the back seat in a bid to discourage him, but to no avail. In fact, it seemed to spur him on further. He obviously thought I was simply playing 'hard to get' — said he liked a girl with spirit! Right, I thought, you have had sufficient warning you sad old pervy. I'll show you spirit!

As usual I took my seat at the back of the bus and one by one the other passengers were dropped off at their respective stops in the villages along the way. We were coming in to the particular point in the journey where this uncouth cradle-snatching slob usually stopped the bus and came to be repulsive next to me. In fact he had already started his awful one-way double-entendre-filled idle chatting from his driving seat, keeping his eyes on the road at this time and smugly speculating to himself what it would be like to have a passionate affair with a sixteen-year-old. So engrossed was he with his own vile little fantasy that he didn't notice me creep from the back seat on all fours down the aisle between the seats. He was still fantasizing out loud when I took my cigarette lighter from my pocket, still on all fours at the base of his seat and set light to the bottom of each of his trouser legs. I thought that his ankles would get a little warm and that there might be a spot of slapping at his own legs to beat out a few little flames. However, I had not taken into account that these particular trousers were made of that wonderfully flammable man-made fabric NYLON. Spectacular is not the word for the ensuing inferno. Although over within a few seconds, his very comical panicking and tearing at his trousers was hysterically funny. He managed to get them off to reveal some very unsexy 'thousand-wash-grey' granddad Y-fronts. Obviously he was unable to walk through the village to his house without his trousers, so after he had put them out with the fire extinguisher by the side of his seat and picked the majority of the crunchy melted bits off the trouser legs he put them back on. They looked very Robinson Crusoe – the sort of singed-smelling brown Bermuda shorts which finished just below the knee.

I seek forgiveness not from this vile suggestive pervert who made many a journey less than pleasant and quite frightening, but from this man's poor wife who must have had to swallow a pretty far-fetched explanation when he got home and who probably had a hell of a sewing job on in order to send him back to work next day decently clad. Also, if he had to have any hospital treatment for the minor burns on his legs, I seek forgiveness from the nurses who would have had to witness his hideous legs and his hideous pants. If this has in any way clouded their perception of men, I am truly repentant. Just as a brief footnote, fate would have it that thirteen years on I now live in the next village to Harby and it's even more of a hick town – this should be judgement on me in itself.

Planet Earth

Dear Simon,

I am writing to you to relieve my conscience of a terrible burden. I did this terrible deed eight years ago.

I used to do a milk round, and I was doing well at it until one day I knocked the handbrake as I was getting out of the van to deliver a few pints.

I didn't notice my mistake until I was up the drive of the house I was delivering to. I heard a noise and turned, only to see the van rolling down the hill and then crashing into a brand-new car. I was literally 'up the garden path'. My boss came running up swearing and I ran down to the van in shock. Twenty-five crates of milk, a van worth £4,000 and a brand-new car were write-offs.

Then I formed an evil plan. I shouted. 'There they go! I saw them! I thought they were mucking around by the van!' I then claimed to have seen two paperboys messing around by the van, and as it was dark no one was any the wiser. My boss went fuming to the paper shop and demanded that the shop owner pay for the damage.

The result was that the two paperboys who delivered in that area were sacked without wages, my boss had to wait three days for a new van and lost most of his customers, the owner of the car (who had just bought it and got a pittance of insurance) had to buy another car (not such a good one), and I retired the next day.

I hope the car owner, the customers who got no milk, the milkman, the paperboys and the shop owner who had to deliver the papers himself for a week, can find it in their hearts to forgive me.

Yours,

Mr X

Dear Sacerdotal Simon,

Whoops! I'd better confess for I have taxidermally trans-
gressed. Two years ago my next-door neighbour decided that she
needed a break from her secretarial job in Ipswich and booked
a ten-day holiday in Belgium. Before she left she asked me if
I would mind keeping an eye on her house, watering her plants,
etc. while she was away. I said that I would, so she left me
her back-door key.

Now, there are two things about this neighbour that you
should know – she never misses an episode of 'Coronation
Street', and about a year and a half before this little event
took place she began to collect stuffed animals. Up to this
point she had bought three, a mallard, a pheasant and a fox –
all of them fellers. Although I don't particularly like the
thought of storing dead animals in a living room, I had nothing
against her little collection. That is, until I saw her peering
over the hedge at my cat and two kittens that were snoozing in
the sun on the lawn – she had a sort of 'Ooooh, they'd look
great on my mantelpiece' expression on her face. It was at this
moment in time that I decided to adjust the woman's attitude
towards little living, fluffy creatures.

My chance came while she was on holiday. I entered her house
and, after eating a packet of crisps which I found in her
pantry, I removed the ex-fox that was running across the top
of her television in a state of non-animation. I placed the
poor chap in a black bin-liner, tucked him under my arm and
took him to my workshop. My workshop is my pride and joy – it
is here that I make and mend all kinds of electrical gadgets,
remote control vehicles, etc. Indeed, I am a bit of a wizard
when it comes to electronics.

In my workshop I set about 'operating' on the fox – a project
that took me the best part of two days. After this time I had
successfully loosened the joints of the creature and given the
tail a certain amount of flexibilty. I had also inserted a
simple system of small electrical motors which would drive an
even simpler lever system into the parts of the fox whose days
of cunning were no more. Are you getting the picture?

I returned the fox to its deathly still position of running

across the top of the television, plugged it in and set the timeswitch that I had, at considerable expense, purchased for this very cause. It was perfect, the lead and wall socket were hidden behind the telly, and the fox, despite my adjustments to its inner self, had not visibly changed. It was Wednesday morning. She, the collector of former furry animals, would be returning that afternoon. 'Coronation Street' would begin at 7:30 that evening; the timeswitch was set for 7.45.

I sat in silence at home, listening to the wall. At precisely 7:45 I heard a scream that would wake the dead, followed by a rather worrying crash. I dashed across to her house to see what had happened. She was sitting in an armchair crying and shaking, the fox had stopped whirring, squirming and twitching, there was a trail of coffee across the carpet, leading from the armchair to the telly, and a mug nestled in the television where the screen used to be. In between hysterical sobs she explained that her fox had 'come back to life' and she thought that it was 'going to get her'. I poured her a stiff drink and told her to go to her bedroom and lie down. As she was going upstairs she asked me if I would mind 'getting rid of the animal'. I grinned, told her that I would kill it for good this time and, while she was upstairs, I removed the timeswitch, electrical lead and the star of the show himself. Two weeks later she had sold Mortis the mallard and Frigid the pheasant, and she hasn't bought any taxidermial terrors since.

OK, what's the verdict? Am I forgiven?

Dear Reverend Father,

My confession revolves around an event that took place back in the balmy summer days of June last year. My mate John and I share a speedboat, and our summer relaxation is the environmentally vicious sport of water-skiing. Great fun, but as you can appreciate rather expensive, so the usual thing is to invite along some more bodies to enjoy a day out, and contribute to the costs of the day.

On the day in question, the guests were, well, we'll call them Pete and Liz: friends of John from a previous job. I knew them both, but had only met them twice before. Pete and Liz were both vegetarians, and duly arrived at the lake in the regulation 2CV, with the usual 'Nuclear power, no thanks' sticker in three different languages on the boot. More fun ensued when Pete removed his clothes to reveal a pale undernourished body, in desperate need of some protein. The spare wetsuit was not exactly a good fit, and to say he rattled in it would be an understatement. The day went very well, and as the sun set we set off tired and hungry back to John's house where all was ready for a barbecue.

Why is it, that the length of time it takes to light a barbie is directly proportional to how hungry you are? It took ages, which gave us plenty of time to sink a few G+Ts and review the day's activities. Eventually after assistance from a Hot Air Paint Stripper the charcoal was alight and the cooking could begin, which was just as well because we were all feeling quite light-headed after drinking on an empty stomach. I took control of the cooking, and unwrapped the sausages, beefburgers, and steaks that had appeared from John's fridge. Liz then handed me a pack of frozen veggie burgers. She averted her eyes from the cold meat on the plate next to the barbecue, and requested that I keep her food separate during cooking. I said that I would try, and she returned to her carrot juice.

All was going very well on the barbie, the sausages were fizzing away, the steaks were almost finished, and the beefburgers had been turned once and were doing nicely on the other side. Just then John came over to check on the progress, as it had been about an hour and a half since we had arrived back from the lake, and he was feeling very hungry. 'All looks good to serve in about two minutes,' I said, 'except for Pete and Liz's veggie stuff, still looks a bit pale to me.' 'Blimey, it does,' said John. 'Move them over the flame.' This I did, the flame licked the veggie-burgers for about a minute, I turned them over hoping to see some change in their complexion but they were as pale as Peter's chest. 'We can't have this,' said John. 'We're all hungry.' 'There's not much I can do about it is there?' I replied.

In an instant the same evil thought came into both our minds. I looked at John, John looked at me. 'We couldn't,' we said in unison. 'We could!' we agreed.

John stood guard and kept an eye on Pete and Liz. I picked up a sausage with the tongs and held it over the veggie-burgers and pricked it with a fork. The juices flowed, and I duly covered each veggie-burger with a good coating of pork fat. They really started to sizzle, and in a minute or two went a lovely brown colour. 'Food's up!' I shouted, and the now ravenous hordes descended onto the succulent food on offer. Pete and Liz took their two dark golden veggie-burgers, some salad, and started to eat. I eyed John nervously, but we both choked back a laugh when Liz remarked to Pete that they were the best burgers that she had tasted, and she would buy some more next week!

Bournemouth

Dear Father Mayo,

As a keen horsewoman one of the main activities of the summer was to compete in as many shows as possible. After an especially disappointing season when I was twelve . . . well, OK, fourteen actually, I decided at one such show that I would get my own back on a fellow competitor who had gloated over my horse, Bumbles, and me, with her winnings all season.

It was a fairly big show and I was just putting the final touches to my horse when she strode past looking immaculate and all ready for her first class which was 'Best turned out horse and rider'. She was always sickly-sweet towards me which meant you could never be nasty to her. Anyway she stood watching me for a moment and seeing I was in my usual panic, asked if she could help at all. In that second the evil plan flashed through my mind and the devil within started tittering. 'Actually', I said, 'you could pick her feet out for me' (a cleaning method – for all non-horsey people). 'How about tying her up over there on the straw which has been scattered about?' Amanda readily agreed. Puffing out her little chest with self-importance she did as she was asked. Now Bumbles has a habit of lifting his tail and expelling – shall we say – solid matter soon after he is led on to clean straw. Only in summer, when the grass is rich, it is not quite so solid (and very green).

I busied myself putting away bits and pieces into the horse box whilst watching from the corner of my eye. Bumbles performed right on cue, whilst Amanda was bent double, peering down and cleaning with gusto, Bumbles' hind right foot. The shriek that she emitted caused a chain of events that upset more people than you can imagine. A class going on nearby took fright and two ponies backed into and sat on a jump, another horse broke free from where he was tied up and caused havoc, dispersing a crowd within a few seconds!! And someone else dropped a tray of drinks. However, the best sight of all was Amanda. She hadn't sprung away from Bumbles quickly enough and most of it was in her hair, some was smeared on her blouse but a lot of it was on her whiter-than-white jodhpurs. Meanwhile, I had slumped against the horse box having absolute hysterics – I can honestly say I have never seen anything quite so funny before or since. I know it was a bit mean so I beg forgiveness not only from Amanda but all the people whose day I messed up at the show, especially from the bloke who probably spent a tenner getting the drinks only to drop them all.

Very hopefully yours,

Andrea

Cardiff

Dear Simon,

This holiday confession concerns that great student pastime, Inter-railing. (For those not aware of it, Inter-rail is a rail ticket which gives anyone up to a month's unlimited travel throughout most of Europe.)

I was travelling with three others: Anthony, Rachel and Helen. We had travelled throughout Holland, Belgium, Germany and Austria, and were now heading into Switzerland, aiming for our next proper stop, Lyon in central France.

We arrived at Zürich and had to wait for four hours for our connection. It was on one of the platforms that we literally bumped into a group of Inter-railers from Guildford. Almost immediately, we realized that we just had to get away from these prats. As we had time to spare, we decided to have a quick walk around Zürich, but unfortunately, the other group attached themselves to us and followed us around.

Eventually we went to a café for a drink. The other group was made up of three lads: Mike, Gary and Wayne. We found out that they supported Arsenal – not a good start . . . They had struggled around eastern Europe and had travelled from Greece up through Italy. They couldn't speak any foreign languages and had been a general nuisance wherever they went. They were also heading for Lyon and then north to catch a ferry.

We put up with them talking Tony Adams, etc., all the way to Lyon on the train. Try as we might, we couldn't get rid of these human leeches – they even came to our campsite and set up their tents next to ours! That evening they continued to irritate us, making sexist comments about the two girls in our group (generally to do with kitchens . . .). Their eating habits were disgusting and later they got drunk on cans of lager (which we picked up later). In the night while we slept, Mike, Gary and Wayne thought it would be hysterical to pull out our tent pegs. To misquote Queen Victoria, 'We were not amused.'

By the next day, we could stand it no more, so Anthony and I worked out a plan. Since we were able to speak French, we were able to convince the lads that we would be on different trains – us direct to Dieppe, them direct to Boulogne. In truth, both groups could have travelled to Paris together and then separated. However, Simon, this is not what I am confessing for . . .

We walked to Lyon station together and booked their seats for them. The train arrived and they were soon on their way, having swapped addresses. We left an hour later.

Our whole group would like forgiveness for the following:

1. We are sorry for making up addresses for them to write to – but the idea of Mike, Gary and Wayne suddenly turning up on the doorstep was too much to bear.
2. We are sorry for making fun of Arsenal – but it had to be done.
3. But, last and definitely not least, Anthony and I would like to apologize to Gary, Wayne and Mike for sending them to Bologna in northern Italy instead of Boulogne in northern France. . .

I hope you can forgive us, taking into account their manners, general behaviour and their love of Arsenal 'football' club.

Yours hopefully,

Dave

Sittingbourne

Dear Father Simon,

To set the scene my friend, whom we'll call Bob, failed to achieve the required grades to enter medical school, so in search of a career with 'action' he applied for and successfully joined our local county constabulary.

After four months' intense training the obligatory attendance at an autopsy was called for at a local hospital. On hearing this Bob enthused at the opportunity to view some real 'action'.

During the previous four months one particular member of the class had been the ultimate pain in the proverbial, and a loud one at that, quickly obtaining the nickname Blackwall Gob. Blackwall had quickly started his boasting 'I've-seen-it/done-it-all-before . . .' attitude when he was informed of the pending hospital outing.

Both Bob and the instructor of the class had both quietly aired their opinions of what they thought of Blackwall, and so seeing the mortuary visit as a perfect opportunity to verbally castrate the mighty mouth, started plotting. The day arrived and 26 pasty faces alighted from the police van and entered the mortuary department. The doctor scheduled to lecture the group was still finishing off a customer (sorry!) and so the group was asked to wait in an anteroom behind the main theatre. This room led off to the refrigerated room where the body drawers were situated. Bob and the instructor pulled Blackwall to the side and asked him if he would like to help play a joke on the rest of the unsuspecting class. Of course he grabbed the chance. They said he should lie in one of the body drawers with a sheet over him and then when the doctor showed the class around he would pull out the relevant drawer and then Blackwall could sit up and frighten the rest of the class. We duly stripped him of his uniform down to his Y-fronts and laid him to rest!

To make it clear to those of you who are unfamiliar with a mortuary drawer, when the drawers are pushed back in, the fridge is open plan. That is to say when Blackwall was pushed back in, he could look either side of him and see all the other 'residents'!

They assured Blackwall that he would only be in there for two or three minutes . . . They knew that after ten minutes one of two things would happen – either he would start shouting and banging to get out, or he would mutter something like 'For goodness sake, hurry up . . .'

Well the latter occurred, as planned, and this is where a strategically placed second person came into play! Another 'keen to quieten Blackwall' candidate had offered his services. He lay in an adjacent drawer and in reply to Blackwall's lonely (or so he thought) mutter replied, 'Cold in here, isn't it?'

To say that the screams from Blackwall Gob could have woken the dead is not an overstatement, and to say he was introverted after the prank is perfectly true.

I would like to beg forgiveness for Bob and his instructor, but also for the likes of myself who thinks the prank hilarious but quite rightly cruel.

Yours requesting absolution,

Natalie

Cardiff

Dear Father Simon,

Your 'confessional' has given me the chance to get a great weight off my chest.

Four years ago, I was at university studying for a Chemistry degree. A friend of mine on the same course, Phil, decided that he wouldn't bother coming in for the early morning lectures because he was too lazy. I, of course, went to all the lectures and would lend him my notes to copy.

Unfortunately, he kept on losing my notes so I decided to photocopy them for him instead. However, a plan started to form – why should I have to go to all the early lectures so Phil could get all the notes. So, as I photocopied the notes for him, I would omit certain important paragraphs and equations, or change them so that they were incorrect.

By the end of the first year, Phil had over two hundred pages of work that was completely wrong. The first year exams came – I passed and Phil failed miserably. He just couldn't understand it. Fortunately, he would have another chance in the October resit, so that he could go into the second year.

I saw him just before the first resit to wish him good luck and he said he felt very confident. He had been revising for about eight hours a day since he had failed. Well, the results came out and Phil had failed even more miserably and was thrown off the course.

According to his last letter to me, he has managed to get a job as a milkman (lots of getting up early!). It's sad to think that he had once had aspirations of running a multinational company.

Well, Phil, I must confess that the reason that you're not where you once hoped to be is my slightly inaccurate chemistry notes. Can you forgive me?

Yours hopefully,

David

Cockermouth

Dear Simon,

I spent eight years in the Royal Marines, and it will come as no surprise to you when I say that the humour of the Forces in general can be rather harsh and cruel sometimes. It was only after leaving the Forces and attending teacher training college that I found that some of the things that had often had myself and fellow marines in stitches, failed to raise even a smile when told in civilian company. Gradually, as is always the case with us social beings, I learned to adapt and to relate different tales and to laugh at different things. But this one true story that I am about to tell you simply refused to die a death in my memory, and has haunted me for over twenty-five years.

I was awaiting the start of a specialist training course, and was given the job of unit postman, a job shared between two NCOs, and a role that always made whoever was doing it very popular. People were always dropping in to our office to see if they had any mail, and Ben and I made everyone welcome, enjoying the chat and a laugh. Some people visited more often than others, and one young officer, who was a fresh-faced twenty-year-old, became a daily visitor, telling us about home, and his aspirations in the Marines. He was so keen and eager about his choice of career that his enthusiasm made us poke fun at him sometimes, for it was implicitly understood that we should not show too much enthusiasm for the Corps. Fate, as always, deals cruelly with those who have not learned the lesson about having a circumspect approach to the future, and our young officer appeared one day with a long and sorrowful face. It seemed that for medical reasons he was not to be allowed to continue his career, and he was to leave the Corps within a couple of months. Ben and I could have instantly named two dozen or more marines that were desperate to get out, yet here was fate decreeing that the keenest commando we'd ever met should leave – how sad, how savage, how ironic.

It called for a night to remember, a night that our young friend could always look back on, to tell his children about one day, of how he painted Plymouth red in the company of two good mates who were sorry to see him go. So ashore we went, a few days before he was due to go home, and by 11 pm his eyes were glazed, and his legs no longer working. I won't bore you with the tawdry, bawdy details, but it was nothing new really, a poor man's 'Carry On . . .' script. However, the climax of the night which Ben and I had dreamed up, and which we'd been hysterical about in anticipation several times, finally arrived. In the small hours of the morning we sat him down in the tattoo parlour and as he looked down on his arm in a befuddled and puzzled way, the needle traced out in glorious Technicolor '43 Commando Royal Marines' with an upraised dagger central to the design. What a great night – a good few beers, and a story that we could tell and re-tell that would always raise a laugh.

Next morning Ben and I were on our rounds delivering the mail to the various offices, when we saw our young, very hung-over friend appear with two fellow officers, who were providing both physical and moral support for him. With no beating about the bush one of them approached us and said, 'That was a rotten thing to do last night.' I played the complete innocent. 'What do you mean?' 'I mean getting him tattooed,' he replied, somewhat belligerently. 'Oh, the tattoo,' I said. 'That's nothing to worry about, it's only a transfer. It will wash off.' Our young friend's face lightened, and his shoulders looked as though a great weight had been lifted from them. 'Will it?' he asked, scarcely able to believe his ears. 'No,' said Ben, and we fell about once more, delirious with the humour of the situation.

Many is the time I have thought about this over the years, and I have latterly truly and earnestly hoped that that tattoo did not cause him too much sorrow after he left the Corps. It has taken me a long time to sit down to expurgate the memory of the deed, but it was a great night out.

Sin City,
Derbyshire

Dear Father Mayo,

We feel it is time to confess to our terrible sin that we committed about a year ago.

It all began when one of us was seeing who she thought was 'Mr Right', although I thought this smarmy, pretentious creep was 'Mr Wrong'. His name was George and he worked in the offices of a computer showroom, although he kept bragging he was worth much more. He had applied for a particular job with a well-known High Street bank, which would bring him promotion and better pay.

He had attended an interview and was sure he was the best man for the job. Now he had achieved greater status in his career he felt my friend was no longer good enough for him, and went as far as telling her so. This obviously left her upset and wanting revenge – so we started plotting.

The next day I rang George explaining that I was the personnel manager from the branch 'he would be working at'. I went on to tell him he had got the job and to hand in his notice at the firm he currently worked at, as he would start work in three weeks time. I also told him to buy suitable clothes and preferably a real leather briefcase. He would start work at 10.30 am and so was asked to arrive at the front desk at 10 am to introduce himself to the manager.

In the weeks that followed we discovered he had immediately given up his job in favour of his 'new career'. We also learned he had been spending his nights in, saving up for a new suit and a real leather briefcase, costing around £200.

About 9.55 am on the morning George was due to start his new job, it just so happened we had run out of money so we called in at our local bank. Just before 10 am the doors opened and there was George, modelling a brand-new designer suit and clutching a leather briefcase. As we hid behind the leaflets he confidently strode to the front desk and asked for the manager.

When the manager appeared George shook him firmly by the hand and loudly announced himself as the new management trainee due to start today. The bewildered bank manager made his excuses to check this, leaving a less-confident George nervously clutching his briefcase.

The bank manager's reappearance confirmed that George had been mistaken and the job was not his after all. After much argument with him, George was repeatedly told that his was a good application but the job had gone to someone else. George was then requested to leave.

We would like to confess to the bank manager – yes, it was those two giggling girls behind the mortgage leaflets that had played the prank. We would also like to confess to George that it was us and we are very sorry you lost both jobs, your social life, your savings, your dignity and your pride, (still the leather briefcase does look nice whilst you collect your UB40).

But most of all we would like to apologize to the bank 'that likes to say YES' – but this time said NO.

Can we be forgiven for our sin as we brought pleasure and amusement to a few bored cashiers and customers in that bank on that morning?

From,

Two little angels

Sheffield

Dear Simon,

I have to confess to a most heinous crime against a poor unfortunate fellow soldier back in 1975. When I joined in 1974, army barracks still had four and eight men to a room so if you wished to get on with your roommates you kept your area clean and didn't disturb the others at night when they were sleeping.

I was based at Athlone barracks in Germany and our room had the misfortune to be blessed with a chap none too clean, frequently drunk at night and a lover of heavy metal after a session on the local beer. Now we weren't exactly teetotallers ourselves and we like a bit of headbanging music as well, but he was a regular nuisance. So one Sunday night our hero turned up banging into everything that couldn't move, switched on his stereo complete with Led Zepellin II and collapsed into his pit, soon to be in the land of Nod. Making sure he was fast asleep we tucked him up nice and snug and then carefully carried him out, bed and all, and put him in the centre of the parade ground. A mate of ours then put an instant tattoo on his forehead. Hoping the sentries would not report seeing him we retired to sleep and to await further developments.

In the morning after breakfast the whole regiment was quietly standing at ease, all in neat ranks surrounding our hero, who was still oblivious to anything but his soon-to-be-interrupted sweet dreams. So at the appointed hour the officers approached led by the RSM! Spotting our hero the RSM marched up to the bed and tapped him gently on the shoulder asking him if he had had a nice kip. Fighting his way through an alcoholic haze it took Henry the brain cell five seconds to realize that being woken up by the RSM was not normal army procedure. Leaping out of bed and trying to stand to attention whilst turning a whiter shade of pale was a sight to see.

The RSM not very kindly enquired why our hero was on the parade ground and would he please accompany him to the guard room quick march left, right, left, right. Imagine my amazement when I discovered that it wasn't hot buttered scones and sweet tea they were marching off to, but our hero had a regime of dirty, menial jobs with nasty men shouting at him for a week.

Contrary to the belief that soldiers volunteer easily no one admitted to depositing said person on sacred parade ground so after all these years I would like to beg forgiveness and absolution. Especially to my comrade in arms and possibly his poor wife who may wonder why her husband has nightmares concerning a regimental sergeant major and a bed.

Yours sincerely,

Richard

Dear Simon,

After spending the weekend at a party with some friends in Bristol I have decided it is time to confess a recent misdemeanour. Not because I am worried, but because my former friends were absolutely horrified that I could possibly commit such a wicked crime.

Having spent a harrowing week at our Head Office in Leicestershire, I was at the railway station, aiming to be home for 5.45 pm (sorry, I mean 17.45, as per our Company regulations), when I heard a booming voice in the distance. 'Hey, boy, hey you, boy!'

I ignored the commotion, as I knew this comment would not be aimed at me. How could anyone in their right mind possibly refer to me, Dave the Rave, as a boy, when everyone knows I'm a man!

I carried on perusing my newspaper when I felt a tugging at my Giorgio Armani designer jacket. I glanced across casually to my right, to see a middle-aged country lady standing there in twin set and pearls awaiting a reply. She then said, 'You, boy, yes you, boy. I'm talking to you! Look at me when I'm talking to you!' At this, I took great offence; how could any woman call be 'boy', let alone twice in the same sentence?

'Is this the train to Exeter?' she asked. My devious little mind started to tick over. 'Yes,' I replied with one of my most provocative smiles. 'Shall I help you with your bags?' 'Yes,' she said, and stomped off in the direction of the train. I placed her bags in the luggage rack, made sure she was comfortable in her seat and made my exit from the carriage to await my train.

Yes, you've guessed it, she was soon speeding not to Exeter but on the InterCity heading north, first stop Sheffield. All I can say is, no one calls me 'boy' and gets away with it.

I cannot believe my friends can't find it in their hearts to forgive me, can you? I don't care if the lady in question can't forgive me, but I know if you can forgive me, my friends will in time.

I am now referrred to as 'Dave Boy'. I don't know if I can handle this.

Yours sincerely,

Dave Boy

Tenby

Dear Simon,

Whilst in Greece on holiday with my best mate, we found ourselves drinking at a local tavern. We spotted two lovely-looking young ladies sitting outside in the warm sun, and bravely decided to go chat them up.

My mate, who is tall, dark and handsome, obviously had no problem, but I, being short, pale, ugly and balding, had no chance. We chatted for a while, well they did, but my mate completely left me out, feeling like an idiot. He then arranged to meet both the girls later in the evening. He even had them agree to call for him at his hotel room at 7 pm!

I went back to my room, a little despondent to say the least, wondering what to do with my night. I suddenly had an awful, evil and nasty thought. I ran downstairs and out into the little village to find a chemist. I eventually found a shop which sold toiletries, etc. I asked the old lady for a sachet of hair removing cream for my 'wife', and left with a packet, grinning to myself.

I rushed up to my mate's room and let myself in; then carefully squeezed the contents into his shampoo bottle which was almost empty, as he washes his hair twice a day! I then left his room, already feeling guilty. He later returned and, as every other night and morning, washed his hair and showered.

He had rubbed the whole bottle of shampoo-cum-hair-remover all over himself, and had tufts of hair coming away as he dried himself. He shouted from his door for me to come quickly, I ran over, and he was hysterical!

Clumps of hair had come away from his scalp, his eyebrows were thinner, plus most of the hair on his arms was gone, as he'd obviously rubbed shampoo 'all over' if you know what I mean. He began crying, and could not believe what was happening. I felt really bad for what I had done. He thought he'd caught a social disease or that the foreign food hadn't agreed with him.

He spent the rest of the holiday on his balcony while I got to take the two girls out, as he was 'ill in bed'. I had a wonderful evening, with my mate back at the hotel!

After writing this down, I realize that I cannot be forgiven, or can I?

Yours sincerely,

Andy

P.S. His hair has fully grown back now.

'Honestly, it wasn't my fault...'

My 3-year-old son has a number of stock phrases which he uses on a regular rotation system. 'I've done a poo', 'I want to watch Thomas the Tank Engine', and 'I didn't mean to'. The first two of those most of us grow out of, but that last one seems to retain its popularity.

Dear Simon,

I've decided to write to you about something that happened ten or twelve years ago. My dad had his own wholesale toy business, supplying beach balls, teddy bears, buckets and spades, and so on to resorts on the east and west coasts.

One Sunday at about 7am there was a first delivery to Cromer, where there is a very steep slipway down to the beach. Halfway down where fishing boats were launched, there was a little seaside shop. There was quite a bit of stuff to deliver, so Dad decided it was best to reverse down the slipway to it. I was driving, as he jumped out to guide me down. As he was waving me back, doing the 'come on' and 'left hand down' bit, he recognized someone he knew up on the main road and started to wave at him. I looked up the road to see who it was waving back at my dad, and just then I felt a slight 'bump' from the back of the truck. I checked both mirrors and stuck my head out of the window, but, my dad had vanished.

I jammed on the handbrake and jumped out of the cab, thinking I might just have done something my mother would not forgive me for. I ran to the back of the truck and saw I had bumped into a mobile ice cream kiosk, which had been propped up on bricks at one end to make it level on the steep cobbled slope. I say had been propped, as now it was slowly rolling down the slipway with my dad hanging on to the jockey wheel trying to stop it.

I tried to grab hold of my dad, but tripped over the bike chained to the kiosk (for safe keeping) which was being dragged down the slipway, now a little quicker. It was then that I became aware of the loud barking noise coming from inside the kiosk, which was rolling along quite quickly with my dad running behind still trying to stop it.

I just stood and watched, tears gathering in my eyes, helpless . . . with laughter. The kiosk, containing a dog, dragging a bike and my dad down the slipway, had picked up quite a bit of speed in just a few yards. It made quite a splash when it hit the water at the bottom of the slipway.

After all the noise of this charade it suddenly went very quiet (apart from the berserk dog inside the kiosk!). My dad stood up to his bruised and scraped knees in the sea and looked around, then at me. I looked around, then at him. There was no one else about. Without a word spoken we both ran back to the truck, got in and drove off.

The following week there was an article in the local rag about vandals smashing up the seafront, the ice cream salesman went 'bust' because the kiosk fell apart after it was rescued at low tide. The bike got a bit mangled, the shop lost its delivery and one of its main suppliers – my dad – never returned, the dog survived although lived in mortal fear of water and enclosed spaces.

To you all I am very sorry indeed, but it was half my dad's fault. I now live on the east coast and one of my sisters-in-law lives in Cromer.

I don't care if you forgive me, but it teaches my dad a lesson not to throw away my Scalextric set. I am 34 years old.

Jasper

Lanarkshire
Scotland

Dear Simon,

In 1980, two friends, Bob and Hugh, and I attended a Union
Conference in Egham, and stayed for two nights at the local
university. Bob had been suffering from gastroenteritis, and
on the morning we were due to leave, he was unfortunately not
quick enough in rushing to the toilet and, much to his embarrassment, soiled a sheet.

He took the sheet off the bed and at 5.30 in the morning
sneaked down to his car. In the boot of his car, he had a large
HMSO envelope from his work and he crammed the offending sheet
into it.

On our arrival home, we stopped at a small village in
Lanarkshire and ate some chips in a car park next to a Police
Station, which we could see was unoccupied at the time.

Bob burst into laughter and told of his misfortune that
morning. He said that he had a great idea for a laugh. He then
took the large envelope from the boot and squeezed it through
the letter box of the Police Station.

We drove off in a fit of laughter but after 300 yards, Bob
stopped the car with a screech of the brakes. He turned to us
ashen-faced and said, 'Oh my God, my name and address were on
that envelope!'

Belated apologies to the student who lost his sheet, and to
the local constabulary in Lanarkshire.

Yours sincerely,

John

Dear Simon,

As the New Year celebrations fade into memory we find ourselves once again approaching another festival when 'Jocks in Frocks' appear from the woodwork and tartan octopi are dragged screaming into pubs and clubs to remind us why the Romans built Hadrian's wall.

Yes, we are approaching Burns Night.

We haven't had a Burns Night in our local club since 1992 and there are no plans to hold one this year.

My confession and plea for forgiveness date back to January 1992 when, as chairman of the entertainments committee at The Corner House Club, I was responsible for organizing a Burns Evening. With the assistance of our Scottish members and members of the Leeds Caledonian Society an impressive programme was prepared for the evening. The haggis had been delivered from Aberdeen as apparently the sheep up there have particularly tasty hearts, lungs and livers. A piper was organized and the various speakers had rehearsed their parts. Everything had been meticulously planned.

Having previously attended several Burns evenings I was aware that there could be serious and sombre moments and that the ceremony is taken very seriously by our Scottish brethren. The haggis is piped in on a silver tray and this was scheduled for 8.00 pm. At 7.00 pm everything appeared to be going well. The neeps and tatties were cooked and all but one of the haggis had been sliced into portions and stored in hostess trolleys. The club had no catering facilities so, as we lived only yards away, my wife and I had volunteered to prepare the food. The largest haggis had been selected for the ceremony and was simmering away in the kitchen as I took a shower, happy in the knowledge that our work was almost completed.

Then disaster.

'Get down here quickly!' was the scream from the kitchen. Yes, the haggis had split open leaving a large pan of watery grey gunk. As all the others had been sliced we were left with nothing for the Jocks to parade, address, attack and toast.

'I know what we'll do!' said my wife, running to my eighteen-year-old son's room.

'Steven, have you got a condom handy?'

'Yes, what do you want it for?' was the reply.

I stood open-mouthed as my son held the end open whilst my wife strained the gunk and proceeded to stuff handfuls into the dangling condom. They had not witnessed the solemnity of a Burns ceremony and were blissfully unaware of the feelings aroused in the Jocks on such occasions. They were convinced that nobody would be able to tell the difference. I knew differently and broke out into a cold sweat, my body was numb with fear. The vision of a haggis with a nipple on one end and a rubber ring on the other being held aloft on a silver tray before being addressed and sliced with a silver dagger just did not calm me down. It was with mixed feelings that I witnessed the explosion that followed as the last handful of gunk was pressed into the stretched rubber. My wife, son and kitchen were pebbledashed. Panic once again gripped us.

Frantic telephone calls to all our catering contacts finally paid off and we managed to obtain two small individual-sized haggis from a nearby restaurant's freezer.

These were quickly defrosted and rushed across to the club at the last minute. They were tiny and looked far from impressive so it was decided that both should be placed side by side on the silver tray. As I stared at these two spherical offerings my mind flashed back to the stuffed condom. I bit my top lip, wished the Jocks well and left for my seat in the lounge.

The tale was briefly recited to a few friends in the minutes before the grand entrance then the room was awash with tartan and the air filled with the wail of bagpipes.

The evening was not a total disaster as was at one time feared. The Jocks performed very well but I must seek forgiveness from them and the membership of the club for smirking, giggling and crying uncontrollably throughout the entire ceremony, for not eating my supper (I was not alone on that one) and for effectively eliminating Burns Night from our club's future social calendar.

Brian

Wiltshire

Dear Simon,

Please forgive me for I have sinned.

I must go back three years to when I was working as a lifeguard at a certain holiday camp in Minehead in the southwest of England.

At the end of the season everyone who was still there and wanted to go went into one of the local towns to see the carnival and get very drunk. As the time came to get on the coach, quite a few people turned up, including some of my lifeguard mates whom I didn't think were coming.

When we got into town we did the decent thing and headed for the nearest public house. As it was a fairly warm night, we decided to sit in the beer garden to watch the floats go by. After about half an hour and a couple of pints, we thought we had better move on before one of the lads took root. As everyone got up and started heading towards the street I hadn't quite finished my pint, so I took it with me. To get to the next pub you had to walk down the street next to the carnival floats. So there I was, walking down the street next to a carnival float with an empty pint glass in my hand, talking to a mate, when I felt a tug on my jumper. When I looked down, I saw it was a little girl of about five with something in her hand. When I bent down to ask her if she was lost, she said no and dropped about 50p in change into my glass. The next thing I know, there are kids coming out from all over, putting change in my pint glass. When we got near to the next pub, I discreetly vanished and spent my hard-earned money.

I'm not asking forgiveness for just myself, but also for my mates, as we carried on, all of us, from pub to pub with our glasses, walking slower and slower after each stop and going home with as much money as we'd left with.

Mark

Birmingham

Dear Simon,

Being an avid Radio 1 listener, I decided to nag a few friends into going to the Radio 1 Roadshow in Bangor.

My partner and I decided to ask our friends if they would like to stay over at our flat so that we could make an early start to the Roadshow, to which they agreed. Early on the morning, at about 6 am to be exact, I woke to the sound of Radio 1 on my alarm clock radio.

I got up, got ready and kindly made breakfast for what felt like the hungry five thousand but was in fact for just five of us. At about 7 am we were ready to hit the road, and considering the unreasonable hour of day we were all in good spirits. At around 10 am we reached Bangor, having listened to the radio all the way on our merry little journey. Castle Square was the venue for the highlight of our journey, so we were desperately looking out for the Square but to no avail. We stopped our car and asked two or three local folk if they could direct us to our all-important destination, but, they couldn't oblige. At the point of almost sheer desperation, I spotted a local bobby. 'Stop!' I shouted. 'Ask him, he's bound to know.' So we pulled alongside Mr Plod and politely asked for directions to the Roadshow.

'Radio 1 Roadshow?' he said. 'I'm afraid I don't know anything about that. Are you sure it's Bangor, North Wales, and not Bangor, Northern Ireland?'

A deadly silence fell upon us all, the big smiles we wore slowly disappeared. Yes you've guessed it, we were on the wrong side of the Irish Channel!

Since that day I have had to take severe ridicule from my so-called friends and family alike. The most unfortunate thing about the whole experience is I'm embarrassed to admit I'm a travel consultant!

Before I end my letter can you please confirm that the August Bank Holiday Roadshow this year is being held at Sutton Park, Sutton Coldfield, in the West Midlands and that there is no other location on earth that is called Sutton Park?

Yours admiringly,

Dunbartonshire

Dear Saintly Simon,

I was a Lieutenant in the Women's Royal Naval Service until January 1992 and had always participated fully in any special or sporting activity regardless of any talent or aptitude required. It was with some pleasure therefore that I was picked for the team to represent my department in the annual Christmas 'It's a Knockout' competition (they were scraping the barrel by this stage).

The competition was always a fancy dress competition and our team always consisted of 90-100% girls. It was not surprising therefore that we were never able to win the first prize for sporting prowess due, mainly, to the Royal Marines ensuring that everything was twice as difficult by the time we got to it. However, remembering the motto 'It is not the winning that is important but the taking part', we entered every time. To make up for any inadequacies in the physical aspect of the competition we made sure that we would win the Fancy Dress competition and entered in more bizarre outfits each year.

Two years ago *Batman – The Movie* was *the* movie to see and we decided to go as Batman (all ten of us). We had one man, Dave, in the team and he decided to go as Batgirl despite the fact that he had a very healthy growth of beard and hairy legs. As the day of the competition approached the girls and Dave were busily making outfits and we hit on the idea of transporting ourselves from the workplace to the sports hall by Sherpa van cunningly disguised as a Batmobile.

The day of the competition dawned and at lunch time we all dressed up in black Lycra leggings, black T-shirts with the Batman logo emblazoned on our chests, black plastic capes (thank goodness for bin bags) and black masks. We stuck black plastic wings to the side of the Sherpa van, a large Batman logo on the front and wired up speakers to the cassette player so that we could blast the whole naval establishment concerned with Batman music as we made our way up to the sports hall.

At 12.30 precisely we set off from the office to travel one mile up the hill to the sports hall with yours truly driving.

We could only travel at about ten miles per hour as the wings were quite fragile. The music was blasting and we were all hanging out of the windows waving our capes at everybody and everything we passed. You will have guessed that we were determined to make an entrance.

As we drove up the main road of the naval base there was quite a large number of Ministry of Defence Police to be seen, far more than usual. We sang at them as we approached and waved the wings in their direction but the response was what you might call cool! We drove on assuming that the dinner in the police canteen must have been particularly bad that day. We turned onto the road which takes you up the steep hill to the sports hall and were confronted by a large number of senior ratings dressed in their best uniforms, medals and all, lining the streets. By this time I was beginning to suspect that there was something amiss and asked the members of the team if they knew what was happening. No one answered so I continued up the hill at a stately ten miles per hour, music blaring, lights flashing and ten 'Batmen' shrieking at the top of their voices.

We rounded the next corner to find yet more senior ratings and officers in their best uniforms, some of whom were just managing to suppress smiles. I again asked if anyone knew what was up and a little voice from the back said, 'Isn't it someone's funeral today?'

Realizing that the road we were on also took you to the church and the funeral cortege was only minutes, nay seconds, behind us I slammed my foot on the accelerator and screeched up the hill to the sports hall scattering well dressed officers by the wayside. We hid the 'Batmobile' behind some dustbins and sneaked into the competition hoping nobody would notice us which, in hindsight, was a bit naive since ten 'Batmen' could hardly sneak anywhere.

I would be eternally grateful if you could see your way to forgiving me for this grievous sin since it has haunted me since that day.

Yours grovellingly,

Alison

Dyfed

Dear Simon,

I feel compelled to write to you to ask for forgiveness, for a terrible deed I did nearly ten years ago. It still haunts me, even though I have moved out of the area. Simon, I went unpunished for the crime; Fred my mate 'carried the can' and has suffered persecution, harassment and embarrassment ever since.

My local rugby club of Brecon were on tour to Portsmouth to play the Navy which had kindly put us up in its barracks. I was an innocent seventeen-year-old celebrating my birthday on what was my first tour. One of the older, respectable gents of the tour suggested a couple of drinks before we changed into collar and tie for the after-match reception. What a good idea, we said!

Whilst I was changing into my new suit, some evil fiend threw a cup of cold water over my new shirt. I was outraged – this was my eighteenth birthday. How dare they do this to me and spoil my day? I went looking for revenge. On searching the barrack bathroom area, I found one cubicle engaged and I assumed this must be where the fiend was hiding. I found the mop bucket half-full of stagnant water and detergent and, after I furnished it with a few other necessities, I picked it up, tip-toed to the cubicle, shouted 'This will teach you' and threw the bucket over. I then scarpered quick, passing Fred in the corridor.

On arrival at the reception there were many long faces. Some of the boys had gone down the pub and hadn't come back, maybe because I told them it started at 9.30 instead of 7.30, but worse was to come. Somebody had soaked the Mayor of Brecon in his official uniform with chain of office. He was also receiving medical treatment for a head injury sustained by a flying bucket which had also blackened his eye.

I couldn't hold back. I had to say something, but it came out all wrong, I said, 'It was Fred. I passed him running in the corridor.' Fred couldn't defend himself as he was down the pub with the rest of the boys. They believed my story as I was too young to know any different. Brecon RFC paid the cleaning bill but the Mayor is now the Chairman of the rugby club and poor old Fred has suffered on every tour since, until now.

Am I forgiven for this?

Yours faithfully,

Robert

Somewhere in Devon

Dear Saint Simon,

The time has come to 'own up' to the horrible deed I perpetrated many moons ago. I haven't given my real name as the chap concerned is still alive . . . retired, and bigger than me.

The year was 1974. I was still in my apprenticeship, but deemed trustworthy enough to be allowed out on my own. I was training as a domestic service engineer – washing machines, fridges, that kind of thing.

The boss decided to send me to Torquay for the day, as we were short-staffed. I duly trolled up in the only van available, which was unmarked, white and totally clapped out.

Towards the end of the day, I saw another service engineer heading towards me in his very distinctive, marked service van. He slowed down and extended his right arm out of the window to signal a right turn. (He never ever bothered with new-fangled things like indicators.) My immediate thought was, 'He hasn't seen me', my second thought was, 'Brighten up a boring day, have a bit of fun and frighten the living daylights out of Mick.' So I did a 'gimme five' handshake, at thirty miles per hour. Cool! It didn't half hurt. My hand was stinging for hours afterwards. After that, I just forgot all about it.

One week later, the lads from the various depots in Devon arranged a Saturday night out in Torquay (the bright lights of the Southwest). So, there we were, a whole group of men having a good time, when in walked Mick with his whole arm in plaster! He explained that he didn't have a clue what had happened. He recalled a glimpse of a young man in a white van but that was all. His arm was broken in two places, and to make matters worse his holiday had had to be cancelled because he was in so much pain.

Naturally, we all consoled him, and as I handed him a double Scotch, I tried not to blush or look too guilty.

All I can say now is, 'Sorry Mick, you have probably forgotten me and the incident, but if not, FORGIVE ME!!'

Yours,

Bono